COLUMBIA
45 RPM
LYNN ANDERSON
4-45252
2:52
ROSE GARDEN
Marshall
INPUT
VOLUME
TONE
I0824145

KARR
RANGE CO.
BELLEVILLE ILL.
420

Stand By Your Pan

Published by Harper Celebrate, an imprint of HarperCollins Focus LLC.

Note: This book is intended for informational purposes only. The publisher and the author disclaim all liability for any personal injury, property damage, or other loss that may result from the information contained herein or from the use of any vintage cookware. Vintage cookware may contain hazardous materials. Before use, it is the reader's sole responsibility to thoroughly inspect each piece for structural defects and to assume all risks associated with its use, including potential health hazards and compatibility with modern appliances.

Art Direction and Cover Design: Sabryna Lugge
Interior Design: Kathy Mitchell
Lifestyle and Food Photography: Reactor Media
Additional Photography:
Tiffany Forrester: 6, 8, 58, 60, 73, 74, 81, 82, 132, 134, 137, 146, 154, 180, 183, 214, 225, 229, 240, 247
Hannah Dasher: 33, 78, 157
Taran Blanton: 270
Shutterstock: 68, 70, 90, 138, 140, 186, 196, 209, 210, 243
iStock: 110, 159, 184
ISBN 978-1-4002-5288-6 (HC)
ISBN 978-1-4002-5290-9 (ePub)

Printed in Canada
26 27 28 29 30 FR 6 5 4 3 2

Stand By Your Pan

100 EASY AND AFFORDABLE COMFORT FOOD RECIPES
SO GOOD THEY'LL HURT PEOPLE'S FEELIN'S

HANNAH DASHER

TO MY PARENTS, GRANDPARENTS,
AND BRITTANY—THIS IS ALL YOUR FAULT.

CONTENTS

COLUMBIA
45 RPM
MS-2R
NOT FOR SALE
PROMOTIONAL
LIGHT IS FASTER THAN SOUND
BIG BROTHER & THE HOLDING COMPANY

SIDES

SAUCES AND MORE

DESSERTS

PLANTERS
audio-technica
PIONEER
1991
PLANTERS
LIMITED EDITION

Introduction

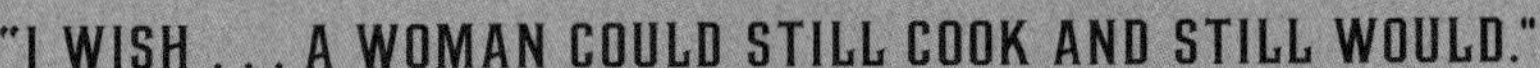

"I WISH . . . A WOMAN COULD STILL COOK AND STILL WOULD."

—MERLE HAGGARD

Just because you're twenty doesn't mean you can't cook like a meemaw. Whether you love to cook or you don't know your butt from a butter knife, this book is for you.

I grew up in the '90s, when we ate home-cooked meals together every night. You sat your ass at the table and ate what was in front of you, and you lived to tell about it. Both of my parents worked full time, yet they *still* made dinner happen. That's the vibe I'm bringin' back.

Single, married, parent, or not—if you can order DoorDash, you can learn to throw down in the kitchen.

There's an art to Southern cooking they don't teach in culinary school. Especially the kind I grew up on in Effingham County, Georgia. Nestled between Savannah and Beaufort, South Carolina, this area is known for its *exceptionally* good food. Eight generations of Salzburgers brought their old-world skills from Austria. When that collided with the bold-flavored influence of the Gullah Geechee African descendants, magic happened. I didn't realize that all soul food wasn't created equal until I left home—but don't worry, I'm here to share some of the secrets . . .

You might've seen videos from my little Nashville home. It's honky-tonk Graceland, frozen in 1972. It's my cozy escape from the music biz (my full-time

job), and it's a nod to the music I fell in love with: country and rock 'n' roll. The kitchen is my safe place when I'm homesick for Georgia. It's stocked with white Tupperware-brand salt 'n' pepper shakers, Merry Mushroom canisters, and vintage Pyrex. It's full of décor from a time before I was born—back when my parents were kids and Tammy Wynette and Loretta Lynn were cooking dinner for their families before hurrying off to play the Opry. Some of my collection even belonged to my heroes. *Stand By Your Pan* is how I keep the nostalgia alive.

Boy or girl, if you wanna up your game in the kitchen, I gotchu, Boo. You can *still* be a rockstar at work and a June Cleaver at home. This book holds the secrets to doing just that—all while saving you time and money!

Life's too short for bad food and boring parties. Let's get to cookin', Linda.

This silver bud vase was given to Hank Williams Jr. and Becky White on their wedding day in June 1977. Their daughter, Hilary, and Ms. Becky gave it to me before Ms. Becky moved back to Alabama.

Vintage "Fish Scale" Pyrex from the Loretta Lynn estate. This was gifted to me by a dear fan, Ms. Jackie Harrison. Loretta's granddaughter Tayla Lynn confirmed, "Yep. That was Mimi's!"

Stock a Soul Food Kitchen

You know why your great-grandmas were badass cooks? Because they saved everything. And not just Cool Whip containers . . . When my great-grandma Ruby died, we found pork chops and rib bones wrapped up in her purses. During the Depression, she stretched the Communion grape juice at Mizpah Methodist Church with homemade wine. She didn't drink, but waste not, want not, right?

I take that same attitude into my kitchen. Not only are they good for your wallet, but these tips will bring deeper flavors to your food and help you cook like a soul-granny.

KEEP YOUR BONES.

Keep your steak and beef-rib bones and store in the freezer (the more meat on 'em, the better). Use these for homemade soups and stock (see Rich Beef Stock, 65).

The same goes for chicken bones. Making a chicken salad? Use your rotisserie carcass for chicken stock (see Rich Chicken Stock, 64)!

And finally, ham bones—my favorite. Please bake a ham (see Sund'y Ham, 127), if only for the sake of freezing it for later use. The ham bone and juices freeze so well and make the *best* vegetables, soups, gravies, and so on. Leave plenty of fat, skin, and meat on the bone. Don't waste anything. Make sure you buy a bone-in, skin- and fat-*on* ham that isn't pre-cut.

KEEP VEGGIE SCRAPS.

The onion skin, the parts of the celery bunch you don't use, carrot peels. All these veggie scraps are great for making stock. Anytime you're using only half of an onion or bell pepper, chop and throw it into a freezer bag for later use. This saves time and money. My wild nana taught me this. (She's the one who got married five times because "I don't like to sleep around." You'll hear more about her as the book goes on.) Nana was rebel enough to allow me to help her cook (and drive) at an early age. She's also the reason I've never had a thigh gap.

Anyhow, make sure you wash your veggies; we're not animals.

KEEP ANIMAL FAT.

Please. Every time I meal-prep chicken, I collect the fat from the bottom of the air fryer to use for later (Lucille Ball saved hers too). Store it in the fridge in a glass ramekin with a tight lid, and use it for gravies and soup bases. Flavor town!

Do this with steak fat (ribeye, brisket, and prime rib trimmings are excellent too). Heat it in the microwave (in said glass ramekin) until all the fat is rendered. Remove any unwanted solids with a clean spoon, then store it in the fridge. It'll make your food taste better than everybody else's. (There's a longer process you could choose, but you've got rockstar stuff to do.) My animal fats keep up to three months. I even keep bacon and sausage grease for frying eggs or making gravies.

STORE FRESH-FROZEN PRODUCE.

Being on the road makes it hard to have a garden. When I visit my home in Georgia, however, gracious family and friends often send me back to Nashville with a cooler of their homegrown produce. We blanch and freeze what we can so we always have delicious produce on hand.

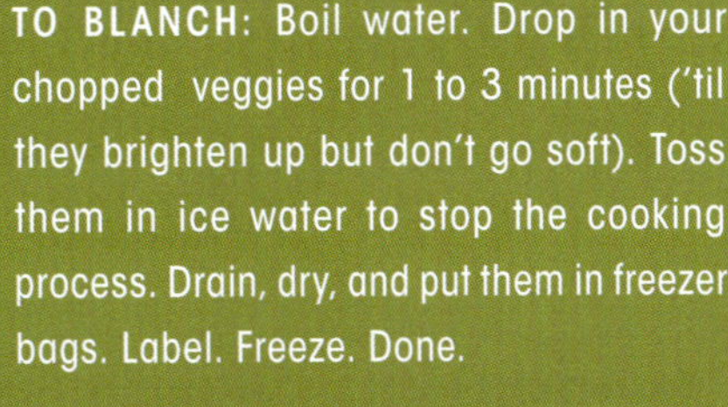

TO BLANCH: Boil water. Drop in your chopped veggies for 1 to 3 minutes ('til they brighten up but don't go soft). Toss them in ice water to stop the cooking process. Drain, dry, and put them in freezer bags. Label. Freeze. Done.

Most fresh produce keeps for a long time in the freezer. I keep blueberries and peaches for a quick cobbler, pie, or smoothie. I keep butter beans and field peas for easy, hearty sides to any main dish. Soups too.

If you have the resources, I encourage you to plant a garden. If you can't, offer to help your friends that do (it's a dedicated task). Help 'em tend it or give 'em nice things, and they'll send you all the fruits and vegetables you need. Try to cook seasonally, but this fresh-frozen method allows you to have ingredients on hand throughout the year.

Ingredients to Always Have on Hand

You're busy, Shoog. Life's expensive! Save yourself a few trips to the store by keeping stuff like this on hand. A great cook is resourceful. You can whip up a feast with little to nothing. Your list may look a little different than mine, so cater it to those who frequent your home.

✳ ✳ ✳ ✳ ✳ ✳ ✳ ✳ ✳ ✳

STOCKING YOUR PANTRY

WHITE VINEGAR

Whether you're using it in soups, sauces, and salads or as a nontoxic household cleaner, you're gonna need this staple.

BAKING POWDER

Use this leavening agent when you run out of self-rising flour. (Just add moisture, and baking powder will release a gas, causing your bake to rise.)

BAKING SODA

Unlike baking powder, baking soda needs to be mixed with an acid (like lemon juice, buttermilk, or vinegar) to give you a good rise on your bakes. You can also use it as an odor eliminator or household cleaning agent. It works miracles to remove coffee stains from your china too.

CANNED TOMATOES

You'll use these for soups, gravies, and sauces, and they can even stand alone as a quick side when paired with rice.

CRACKERS

You never know who's gonna pop over. Keep crackers on hand to fill your appetizer board, to top casseroles, to bread meat to fry, or to make breadcrumbs in a pinch.

EVAPORATED MILK

This will keep a long time in your pantry, and it's a great substitute when you're in a hurry. If your milk's gone bad or a stray cat shows up, you'll need it.

FLOUR

I'm all about White Lily flour. This brand just makes a better biscuit, Brenda. It's softer than its competitors, so if you're using another brand, you'll need to sift it a few times before using it in these recipes.

INSTANT COFFEE

Add this to increase the depth of flavor in baked goods (particularly for chocolate batters), marinades, and tomato-based sauces too.

INSTANT LOW-SODIUM POTATO FLAKES

If you ever need to thicken a soup, sauce, gravy, or stew, add a spoonful of potato flakes. Use them if you oversalt a dish. They'll absorb some of the sodium (a raw potato also works for this). Potato flakes make excellent bread starter. They also keep in the freezer for a long time.

JAMS AND JELLIES

Preserves pair well with cream cheese and crackers for a quick appetizer, or you can serve them with breakfast toast or biscuits. They're a quick and easy way to fancy up a spread when guests drop by.

NUTS

Great for snacking and garnishing baked goods. They keep well in the freezer too.

PICKLED ITEMS

Every good spread needs a little vinegar. Set out olives, pimentos, pickled okra, or homemade pickles—you do you, Linda. Add these to a charcuterie board, or just put them in a glass bowl and make it feel special. Nothing easier!

RICE

Cheap, filling, and built to stretch a meal (and a dollar). Rice soaks up gravy like a champ, makes a heavenly bed for veggies, and lasts longer than most Tinder dates. Ever get your phone wet? Rice to the rescue.

SPICES

These are my favorites I can't live without, but you'll want a lot more. No bland food here, Cheryl.

GARLIC POWDER: No such thing as too much.

CAYENNE PEPPER: Add a little kick. We're not basic.

CELERY SALT: I don't cook a piece of chicken without it.

BLACK PEPPERCORNS: Freshly ground has way more flavor than pre-ground. Get a pepper grinder and grind your own. Course-ground works too.

WHITE PEPPER: It just loves poultry. A little dab'll do ya.

THYME: Dried thyme is a must for meat and potatoes (especially pork and beef). Get thyme leaves, not the ground kind.

CINNAMON: A must for breakfast items, baked items, and chocolate. Add it to coffee grounds when you're feeling fancy.

SUGAR (GRANULATED AND BROWN)

Not only needed for desserts, sometimes a pinch of sugar in your savory dishes makes them taste better than everybody else's. You never know when you or a guest is gonna get a hankering for something sweet or when you'll need to make a goodie to brighten someone's day (like an Easy Almond Torte, 246).

WINE

Just because you're Baptist doesn't mean you can't cook with alcohol, Cheryl. I keep dry red wine, white wine, and sherry on hand for making food richer and for entertaining friends. I buy the six-pack minis so I don't waste a whole bottle when I just need a splash. Always have a bottle or two of Cabernet or a red blend on hand when you serve red meat. Keep Chardonnay, Pinot Grigio, or Sauvignon Blanc to serve with white meat or fish.

STOCKING THE FRIDGE

BUTTER

Salted or unsalted, I'm not a stickler on this, but always have some butter, Shoog. Some baked goods do better with unsalted butter, and sometimes you use it to finish sauces and demiglaces, but don't fret over it. Just make up by adding more or less salt to that recipe.

BREADCRUMBS

They keep forever and make great filler for meats and casseroles, breading for frying, or salad toppings.

CHEESES

I keep sharp and white cheddar, Parmesan, and cream cheese on hand. If company pops over unexpectedly, you'll be able to make a charcuterie board or a quick, easy appetizer, such as my Pimento Cheese (41), Collard Green Dip (39), or Green Olive Spread (46). Keep one firm cheese and one soft cheese at all times to set yourself up for charcuterie success!

CHOPPED ONION

Onions are key for savory recipes, which is why I always have some pre-chopped and ready in my freezer. Frozen will render more liquid than fresh onion, but just allow the liquid to evaporate in the pan while you're cooking. Vidalias work, but I keep yellow onion around, as it's richer in flavor.

LEMONS

Most dishes need an acid. Squeeze lemon on seafood, Dutch babies, chicken, cocktails, and more. It's also handy for eliminating onion smell on your hands after chopping veggies. To extend their shelf life, pop lemons in the fridge or freezer.

PIECRUSTS

Having these on hand in your freezer will save you time. No need to make them from scratch. I like the off-brand ones. They tend to be flakier.

MAYO

I'm a Blue Plate girl, but I cheat on Blue Plate every now and then with Duke's and Kraft. The Bible allows this. Just don't buy light mayonnaise. Ever. Cut the calories somewhere else, Linda.

SOUR CREAM

Sour cream enriches the flavor of sweet and savory dishes; plus, you're gonna make a lot of those Sour Cream Mini Muffins (76).

Kitchen Gadgets You're Gonna Need

Here are some gadgets that'll make your life easier in the kitchen and dining room. (Yes, please use that room too.) Don't worry about buying the latest, most expensive gadgets out there. I mainly use hand-me-downs from old people. The meals eat just the same. Plus, retro items were made to last! Kinda keeps you grounded when you cook with something that belonged to a loved one. Just using the same items they had in that era—when people actually used their dining rooms—helps keep that good energy around.

UTENSILS AND STORAGE MUST-HAVES

BOX GRATER

This is a low-tech way to shred cheese or butter, mince onions, or zest lemons. You'll need one.

CAKE KEEPER AND PIE KEEPER

I prefer vintage Tupperware. These airtight containers allow you to store baked goods so they won't dry out as fast. They also make it easier to travel with said items. Just don't drive like me.

CORNINGWARE OR OTHER LIDDED BAKING DISHES

These come in handy for serving, storing, and reheating food safely. Ask for some hand-me-downs before folks find out how much this stuff goes for at antique stores.

DISPOSABLE ALUMINUM PANS

These are great when you want to take food to a friend or to an event without worrying about anyone washing and returning your dish. As you make your way through this book, you'll also see that I use these often to freeze casseroles or pies.

FOOD PROCESSOR

It's not a must, but it can help you save time. Great for shredding cheese quickly, chopping ingredients, or making piecrusts.

FLOUR SIFTER

When baking, you'll need to pre-sift before measuring any flour that isn't cake flour or White Lily brand. Use this to smooth out the lumps in dry ingredients or to garnish baked goods with a dusting of powdered sugar or cocoa for a professional look.

SANTOKU KNIFE

The shape of this blade (in comparison to a chef's knife) makes for easy chopping. Great for prepping veggies. You can also use it for slicing raw meat or seafood. If you're gonna get one good knife, get this one.

SMALL GLASS RAMEKINS

These are incredibly versatile for serving dips and sauces or dividing items on your charcuterie board.

Or just for melting butter in the microwave. I use 'em every time I cook.

PYREX

Please get rid of those tacky plastic bowls and get these instead. Stock up on all sizes, small to extra-large. Ask your nana if she has some she can part with. Trust me, you want them.

WHISKS

Must have. Use a rubber whisk for nonstick pans. I often use mine instead of an electric mixer—less mess, better biceps.

WIRE COOLING RACKS

One of my secret weapons for baking and frying.

WOODEN CUTTING BOARD

A healthier choice for your meal prep than the plastic ones out there. You'll also want to get a nice wooden board for serving appetizers and charcuterie spreads.

WOODEN SPOON

If you set it over your pot, it'll keep the water from boiling over. Makes a great attention-getter for unruly men and children.

COOKWARE YOU NEED

BUNDT PAN

It's the cake pan with the thing in the center and the fluted sides. You never know when you'll need to make a cake! I use a Bundt pan for my viral pound cakes (see Getchyo' Man Cream Cheese Pound Cake, 223, and Triple-Chocolate Pound Cake, 228) and my Dump Cake for Dummies (224). A Bundt pan is also a great substitute for a salad mold or an ice ring for punch bowls. **NOTE:** My pound cake recipes are written specifically for Bundt pans because of the appearance and texture they render. If you own only a tube pan, that's fine, but you'll need to increase your bake time by 10 to 12 minutes. (Don't forget to slam the oven door after 70 minutes so the cake falls in the center!)

CAST IRON SKILLET

A must. I recommend you start with a No. 3 (8-inch) and a No. 8 (10-inch) skillet. See "Caring for Cast Iron" (22) for tips on how to care for and season your pans.

5-QUART CROCK-POT

That's Southern for "slow cooker," but any brand will do. I have a few Crock-Pot recipes in this book to make life easier.

DUTCH OVEN

It's a must for cooking chili, stews, soups, or stocks. The deep sides also mean you can fry food without the risk of hot oil splattering all over ya.

Caring for Cast Iron

Don't let all the lore scare you, Linda. It's pretty simple. Cast iron's made to last. If you take care of it, it'll take care of you. Stick to these basics:

- If you're making cornbread or biscuits, you'll rarely need to rinse out your skillet. Just wipe out the crumbs.
- Use soap sometimes. If you made gravy or something greasy, use a dab of blue Dawn to break up the grease, and rinse it well. Don't let the pan soak in water. Clean it immediately after use (as soon as it's cooled down).
- Never leave water in the pan, and don't let it air dry. Return it to a warm burner as soon as you rinse it out to allow the water beads to disappear completely.
- Once the pan's dry, use a neutral oil with a high smoke point to finish seasoning your pan. I prefer avocado oil to vegetable oil, but both work well. A little dab'll do ya, though (think Afro-Sheen, not Slip 'N Slide).
- Gently rub coarse salt to remove the rust from your cast iron, should you inherit a rusty skillet. Salt also helps to season the pan. You don't have to do this every time you clean the pan.
- If your cast iron starts to show significant signs of rust or buildup, grab you some steel wool and apply some elbow grease. Rinse well, then heat and oil the pan.

Table Serveware and Décor

Your tableware should not be an afterthought. This is where you can up your game as a hostess and let your personality shine through.

When you're choosing your décor, keep the same color pattern or at least the same color palette on the table if you can. It's soothing and allows the eye to flow over the dishes and focus on the food. You want it to be so pretty that folks'll pull out their phones and take pictures of the table.

CLOTH NAPKINS

We're not animals. I use cloth napkins at every meal to save money on paper products. Throw these in the wash and use them again and again. Plus, they make my guests (and me) feel special . . . because we are. You can search online for inexpensive options, or ask your relatives if they have any they're not using. Or you can cut up an old tablecloth or any fun printed fabric of your choice. Each napkin should measure about 16.5 inches by 16.5 inches. Make sure you have enough material to accommodate the number of people you'll typically host. See pages 28–29 for folding suggestions.

CHINA OR DINNERWARE

The stuff your mom got for her wedding that she never uses? We're using it.

Don't have any china? No sweat! Hit up Goodwill and estate sales, or visit some older family members and ask if they're willing to contribute to your collection. Please do go visit them. Old people are awesome.

Feel free to mix and match. Building a vintage collection is all about using what you have, and collecting things you love. Just find a color palette and stick to it. Less is more. (If you're starting from scratch, try to match your dining room or kitchen colors.) If you mix and match different china patterns, look for pieces similar in size and style. Sticking to the same hues can make your mismatched cabinet and room feel intentional and stylish.

Start by collecting dinner plates and salad plates. Bread plates are great for serving cake and pie. Sherbet glasses are also fun for serving fruit salads and desserts. Ask for soup and dessert bowls for Christmas.

DRINKWARE

Don't spend a fortune! These are easy to find secondhand. Stock up on what you use most.

ICED TEA GLASSES

These are a must. No one's gonna judge you if you serve ice water in them. Water goblets are fun, but they take up a lot of table room and don't hold as much liquid. I'd rather you spend your money on these.

WINEGLASSES

If you're a wine drinker (or host any), make sure you have red or white wineglasses on hand, both if you care to splurge. (I'm still building my collection.)

WHISKEY GLASSES

Obviously, whiskey glasses are great for bourbon drinkers, but I also use them for mocktails, mixed drinks, or even margaritas. Crystal cut glasses are classic and cheap.

ONE TIP: Try to collect glass of the same color. No sweat though. Clear will be easiest to find, and you don't have to use the same brand as your tea glasses. I love the Colony Whitehall glasses from the '60s and '70s. They're cheap and very easy to find. Mine are amber.

SERVING DISHES

You don't need silver service to have a pretty table. Use your Corningware, glassware, or Grandma's Pyrex set to make your food or buffet look presentable.

LARGE PLATTER

You'll need a platter large enough for roasts and meats—something that will display your beautiful meals. Make sure the platter matches some of your serving dishes. It'll take your spread from "men's dirty summer camp" to *Martha Stewart Living* magazine.

LARGE BOWLS

You need at least two serving bowls that match your platter and china pattern. Use that old matching gravy boat if serving gravy or sauce. If you don't have a full china set, try to use the same color serving dishes as your dinnerware, or use neutral serving dishes for your food (like all-white Corningware or glassware). I use my Anchor Hocking glassware in addition to my fine china or everyday china.

TALL GLASS BOWL

Every hostess needs a tall glass salad bowl for serving cold salads, trifles, layered salads, etc.

DEVILED EGG TRAY

If you're gonna serve deviled eggs, get a deviled egg tray. It just makes for a prettier presentation, Shoog. Or look trashy. It's your life.

FLATWARE

Stainless is more affordable than silver by far, but even stainless can get pricey. Hit up a secondhand store or a family friend who's downsizing. Go find you a sugar daddy if you must.

One setting of flatware should include a salad fork, dinner fork, knife, teaspoon, and tablespoon. You should have a minimum of eight settings, but take into consideration the number of people who frequent your home (that way you don't have to wash all your flatware every time you eat a meal). And don't forget serving spoons. Match those too if ya can. I also like to get extra teaspoons and larger tablespoons for sampling and serving foods without cross-contaminating.

You'll need a good set of steak knives for steaks and chops. Look for a vintage set at a thrift store to save money.

CANDLES

Taper candles on your dinner table are always sexy and classic. And they're cheap. Find a pair of candle holders, and that's all the table décor you need. No one has to know they're not sterling. Just make sure the candles match your dining room's color theme.

III
VI
VII
VIII
IX
X

Hospitality Tips

You don't have to break your back to make dinner a fun experience. It should be fun for your guests and for you. I am blessed to know some amazing hostesses, like my mother and my second mother, Ms. Connie Thompson. A longtime resident of Lake Rabun, Georgia (my favorite little fancy place on Earth), Ms. Connie is used to hosting parties of ten or more people. Extremely organized, she's excellent with assigning dishes and tasks ahead of time so that she's free to entertain her guests as they arrive. You don't want your guests to see you in a tizzy. It adds tension to what should be a fun event.

Thompson parties begin with cocktail hour and great music. The meal is delicious and low-maintenance and is usually followed by dancing or games (yes, the whole family clogs—it's amazing). Dishes can wait. It's a missed opportunity not to sit and gather at a meal. That social engagement—away from our devices—is critical for building relationships.

Here are some affordable ways to keep hosting fun and classy.

PLAN AHEAD

Unless you live at Windsor Castle, dinner parties are intimate, so select personalities that will mix well in the room. Consider your guests when planning the menu—food allergies, preferences, and so on.

Your meal should be colorful and balanced. Serve a hearty main, a green vegetable, a yummy starch, and a cold salad to add some color to the plate. Always have dessert. The hostess is typically responsible for providing the main dish, but feel free to lighten your load by assigning side dishes, desserts, and beverages to your guests.

FRESH FLOWERS

Having some fresh, seasonal flowers or greenery in the house (even if only in the bathroom) is an easy way to look like you have your shit together (even if you don't). You can cut something from your yard and place it throughout the house. Don't own a vase? Use Mason jars or pitchers instead.

MUSIC

Music controls the mood of your party. Play some! It breaks the chill in the air. It's also a great conversation piece, so make it vibey, happy, and upbeat. Ballads tend to kill the energy in a room. Reserve the slow songs for the end of the evening.

Select songs with your guests in mind. Create your playlist ahead of time to keep the energy flowing. Long pauses between songs kill the vibe. And you don't wanna be fooling with this while you're trying to entertain.

The music should be loud enough to be heard but not so loud that it interferes with conversation. If you have a guest you trust to DJ, then let them create the mix. As I frequently host other music heads, we turn this into a game. I have each guest queue two songs and pass the phone. (Again, if you feel the energy in the room starting to decline, the music is likely too cheesy or too slow.) Classics are always a great choice. Playlists depend on who you're entertaining and how you want the evening to go. Just remember, you want guests to want to stay and have a good time. Dinner music should be digestible. Vibey and happy but not overpowering. You don't want Rage Against the Machine; stick with Ray Charles's *Modern Sounds in Country and Western Music*, Willie Nelson's *Stardust*, and so on. Post dinner, get turnt. **Check out my playlists on Spotify. I made you one for every occasion.**

THE *STAND BY YOUR PAN* DINNER MIX

"Half as Much"
RAY CHARLES

"Doggone Cowboy"
MARTY ROBBINS

"You Win Again" (1964 version)
JERRY LEE LEWIS

"Don't Get Around Much Anymore"
WILLIE NELSON

"Break It to Me Gently"
BRENDA LEE

"She Caught the Katy"
ALBERT KING

"Strange Brew"
CREAM

"Return to Sender"
ELVIS

"Papa's Got a Brand New Bag"
JAMES BROWN

"You Are My Sunshine"
RAY CHARLES

TABLE SETTING

Up your game and impress your guests, coworkers, future spouse, and their families by setting a proper table. Growing up, my sister and I were assigned the task of setting the table each night at home. Mother used it as a teaching tool. Here are some simple suggestions.

Whether formal or informal, the fork(s) always go to the left of the dinner plate.

The napkin goes to the right of the fork(s), never underneath it. Or put the napkin in the center of the dinner plate if you don't have enough room between place settings.

To the right of the plate goes your dinner knife (blade facing inward), then the spoon(s).

Place drinkware at the top-right of your dinner plate, just above your dinner knife and spoon. The bread plate goes directly above the dinner fork.

CLOTH NAPKINS

Get some or make some, Cheryl (23). Pull them out, especially for guests. It takes only a minute to fold them and it's fun! Plus, your guests'll *really* think you did somethin'. Napkin rings are always an excellent option to make your table look nice, but if you don't have those, here are two classic folds:

OPTION 1: THE PANEL FOLD

Fold the napkin in half, exposing the pretty side. (Make sure the edges meet; we're not animals.)

Then, fold it inward, making four 4 1/2-inch panels. The edge of the end of the napkin should meet or almost meet the last fold.

If your napkin has pretty trim (like lace), flip it over to expose the side with the trim. Make sure all the napkins are uniform. If the napkin doesn't have trim, place it with the hem at the bottom.

Informal settings are more practical for everyday meals.

Formal settings will have more dishes and flatware on the table, relevant to the menu, of course.

OPTION 2: THE PYRAMID FOLD

Fold the napkin diagonally toward you making an upside-down triangle.

Take the left and right tips and fold them down to meet the bottom tip.

Holding the left and right corners, raise to fold the top downward (facing away from you). Then, bring left and right together, inward. Set this in the center of your plate.

ETIQUETTE

Whether you're at Chick-fil-A or a Michelin star steak house, bad manners are such a turnoff. Remember these basics to make you feel confident as a hostess or guest.

FOR THE HOST OR HOSTESS

- Be aware of any food allergies or dietary preferences. If you don't know, ask in advance and plan the menu accordingly.
- Greet your guests upon arrival, and offer them a cocktail or beverage and an appetizer while dinner is being prepared.
- Consider assigning your guests a task when they arrive and or a dish for them to bring so everyone feels included. Plan ahead so you're not stressed when guests arrive.
- Don't make guests wait too long to eat dinner, unless you serve heavy appetizers. Plan your mealtime to be thirty (or so) minutes after they arrive. This also helps you to time cooking your dishes so they're served warm.
- If hosting new acquaintances or someone you've not seen in a while, browse their social profiles before they arrive to brush up on their latest happenings and accomplishments. Taking

genuine interest in your guests really warms up the room. It boosts their confidence and makes for great conversation.

- If you want a reason to see a certain guest again, send them home with their favorite leftovers in a dish they'll have to return.

FOR THE GUEST

- Upon invitation, always ask the hostess how you can contribute to the dinner.
- Bring a hostess gift. Wine, flowers, or a scented candle are always reliable options.
- Gentlemen, remove your hat when you enter the home as an immediate display of respect (also, do so when you greet a woman or when you enter a church). Never wear a hat while at the table.
- Engage in conversation with the other guests. Be curious and make sure to ask questions and listen to the other person's response. People love talking about themselves. Ask how they know the hostess, and go from there!
- Once you take that cute photo of your host's spread, your phone should be on silent and put away—never have it at the table.
- If eating steak or chops, cut only one piece of meat at a time. Rest your knife at the top corner of your plate in between bites. And never ask for steak sauce or ketchup. Well-seasoned meat shouldn't require anything but eating.
- Gnawing the bones is always okay at my house, but follow the lead of your hostess. (Never do this in a restaurant. Ask for a to-go baggie, and clean that bone like a labrador when you get home. Or make some rich-ass stock.)
- Offer to help with cleanup.
- Never ask for leftovers unless the hostess offers. But do ask for the recipe (and I hope it's one of mine).

The Kitchen Is Sexy

For the love, keep it clean (your countertops, your floors . . . you never know where a kiss might lead). It sets the tone for what comes next.

COOKING UPS YOUR GAME. The marrying kind is the cooking kind. Being able to follow a recipe sets you apart from the average Braden or Briley.

LOOK CUTE WHEN YA COOK! Didn't your teacher always tell ya to dress up for test day? Or hell, don't wear a thang but a sexy apron, whether you're male or female (unless you're frying). It'll make ya feel like a rockstar.

HAVE A GOOD PLAYLIST. Mine's called "House-Dancin' Music" because dancing in the kitchen is sexy.

DO THE DISHES. Score points with your partner by doing the dishes when they cook. And vice versa.

MAKE SURE they take you out a few times before you lift a finger in the kitchen. These recipes are special and freaking delicious, and they'll propose after one bite. You don't wanna bring that on too soon. The first time you cook for 'em, prepare what you can ahead of time so it looks like you didn't go to a lot of trouble. Make it yummy and simple—meat and potatoes, a green veggie, a bread. A simple leftover dessert is fine.

Put Love in Your Food

BETTER A SMALL SERVING OF VEGETABLES WITH LOVE THAN A FATTENED CALF WITH HATRED.

—PROVERBS 15:17

The kitchen is a vehicle to love on and connect with people. It's an icebreaker. We may not agree on politics or religion, but we can all agree on a hot biscuit. Food is a great way to bring folks together.

When Daddy built Villalonga, our childhood home, he made the kitchen the largest room in the house ('cause everybody always wound up there).

The kitchen was the epicenter of holidays and celebrations. Plans were made and life lessons were taught in this room. Many memories are seasoned into the walls of my childhood kitchens. I witnessed my parents exchange "I love yous" along with good-morning and good-bye kisses. It wasn't uncommon to catch them sneaking a love note in the other's lunch box. This taught me early on that you have to feed a relationship just like you feed your body.

The nourishment I got wasn't just from the food but from the time we spent as a family around the supper table. Growing up, I took this for granted because everyone I knew dined together as a family at night.

We were expected to bring our full attention. No Game Boys or toys were allowed at the table. TVs were out of sight or muted so as not to distract from family time (though I can still hear Dan Rather signing off in the background from our little black-and-white kitchen TV). We were expected to listen without interrupting and to have appropriate conversation with those present. We took turns leading the blessing. I learned to pray aloud. We felt seen, valued, and included.

Both of my parents were great cooks, so they shared cooking responsibilities. My sister and I had to set the table and help clean up afterwards. (Though Brittany conveniently had to hit the bathroom after every meal). If we finished supper before our parents, we had to ask to be excused. This subtly reminded me who was the head of the household. It gave me a greater respect for the ones who provided and prepared the meal—not just my parents but also for other hosts and hostesses.

I'm not trying to tell you how to raise your own, but so much stems from the family table. You bust your butt to put a roof over your heads and food in your fridge. Why not demand a little more respect for yourself and for all the love you've put into that food? Learning to cook at an early age and helping out in the garden at home made me appreciate the farm-to-table process. I'm more grateful every time I sit down at a table—for the ones who grew the food, the ones who prepared the meal, and the ones who I'm sharing it with.

Food Is a Ministry

FOR I WAS HUNGRY AND YOU GAVE ME SOMETHING TO EAT, I WAS THIRSTY AND YOU GAVE ME SOMETHING TO DRINK, I WAS A STRANGER AND YOU INVITED ME IN.

—MATTHEW 25:35

Cooking is a labor of love. It benefits the cook and the recipient.

If you're going to the trouble to cook, make the full recipe (or double it). Save yourself time down the road! Many of the recipes in this book make enough to freeze or share. If company comes over unexpectedly, I want you to be able to easily whip up something to serve them with just a trip to your pantry or freezer.

You never know when someone will have a death in the family, experience a heartbreak, lose a pet, undergo surgery, have a new baby, or move. There are so many opportunities to love on folks through food. Something that takes you minutes to prepare in the kitchen could make someone's week.

My mama and her friends are good at this. Let's not let this tradition die with their generation. Food is a ministry.

Appetizers

COLLARD GREEN DIP

PIMENTO CHEESE

BETTER-THAN-EVERYBODY'S BUFFALO CHICKEN DIP

BEER AND CHEESE FONDUE

GREEN OLIVE SPREAD

STUFFED ANGEL EGGS

GETCHYO' MAN SCOTCH EGGS

PIZZA DIP, IF YOU MUST

CROCK-POT COCKTAIL MEATBALLS

SPICED CANDIED PECANS

LOW COUNTRY BUTTER SHRIMP

COLLARD GREEN DIP

MAKES 10 TO 12 SERVINGS

Don't underestimate a collard green. Spinach dip is basic. Collards have more flavor. You can fix all of this in one pan. Use leftover homemade greens (see Good Collard Greens, 174), if you wish, but drain 'em well.

5 or 6 slices bacon, chopped, divided

1 small red onion, chopped

2 garlic cloves, finely chopped

¼ tsp crushed red pepper flakes

1 T light brown sugar

4 ounces (½ block) cream cheese, cubed

1 (14-ounce) can seasoned Southern-style collard or turnip greens, such as Glory Foods, well-drained (squeeze to remove liquid)

½ cup sour cream

1 cup grated Parmesan, divided

1 cup shredded sharp Vermont white cheddar, divided

Pork rinds, for serving

1. Preheat oven to 350°F. In a large ovenproof skillet, fry the bacon over medium heat, stirring often, until crisp and browned, about 7 to 8 minutes. Remove the bacon from the grease and place on a paper towel–lined plate. Reduce heat to medium-low and cook the onion and garlic in the drippings until softened, about 3 to 4 minutes. Add red pepper flakes and brown sugar.

2. Add the cream cheese and greens, and cook, stirring often, to melt the cream cheese. Stir in the sour cream.

3. Reserve two tablespoons of bacon, two tablespoons of Parmesan, and two tablespoons of cheddar to sprinkle over the dip later in the recipe. Then add the rest of the bacon, Parmesan, and white cheddar to the skillet.

4. Bake the dip in the same skillet until bubbling, about 25 minutes. Sprinkle reserved Parmesan, white cheddar, and bacon on top. Serve with pork rinds.

PIMENTO CHEESE

MAKES 10 TO 12 SERVINGS

This is always the centerpiece of my "chatta-hoocherie" board. It's also a standard condiment in my home. Spread it on a Cathead Biscuit (72), Sour Cream Mini Muffins (76), Buttermilk Cornbread (71), thick-sliced bacon, celery, or my favorite—Grandma's 14-Day Sweet Pickles (200). Trust me. Naysayers come back for seconds (and fifths).

3 ounces cream cheese

⅓ cup grated Parmesan

1 tsp garlic powder

½ tsp salt

½ tsp freshly ground black pepper

¼ tsp cayenne pepper

Heavy pinch of sugar

¾ cup (6 ounces) freshly shredded sharp Vermont white cheddar

1 cup (8 ounces) freshly shredded sharp cheddar

1 (4-ounce) jar diced pimentos, drained well

½ cup mayonnaise

1. In a microwave-safe mixing bowl, heat the cream cheese for 20 to 30 seconds.

2. Mix in the Parmesan, garlic powder, salt, black pepper, cayenne, and sugar until combined. Stir well to distribute evenly. Add the white cheddar, sharp cheddar, pimentos, and mayo. (Stir carefully so your cheese stays pretty.) Add more mayonnaise (conservatively) to reach desired consistency. Best if chilled a few hours or overnight.

Keeps up to 7 days in the fridge in an airtight container.

CHEF'S NOTE

For best results, do not use pre-shredded cheese. Buy block cheese and shred it yourself (I use a food processor to save time).

BETTER-THAN-EVERYBODY'S BUFFALO CHICKEN DIP

MAKES 10 TO 12 SERVINGS

Girls my age like to fix this with canned chicken—*gross.* If you need to do it in a dash, grab a rotisserie! Your guests are worth the effort.

2 T rendered chicken fat or butter

½ cup chopped celery

½ cup chopped red onion

1 pound boneless, skinless chicken tenderloins, cut into 1-inch pieces

½ tsp salt

½ tsp coarsely ground black pepper

½ tsp garlic powder

8 ounces (1 block) cream cheese, cubed

1 cup sour cream

1 ½ T dry ranch dressing seasoning mix

¾ cup buffalo sauce, such as Texas Pete or Louisiana Hot Sauce

1 T honey

1 heaping cup (8 ounces) shredded low-moisture mozzarella, divided

1 heaping cup (8 ounces) shredded sharp cheddar, divided

Celery sticks and crackers, for serving

1. Preheat the oven to 350°F. In a large ovenproof skillet, melt the chicken fat over medium-low heat. Cook the celery and onion until tender, about 4 minutes. Increase the heat to medium, add the chicken, and sprinkle with salt, black pepper, and garlic powder. Stir occasionally until the chicken is cooked through, about 6 minutes.

2. Transfer the chicken and vegetables to a food processor and pulse until coarsely chopped (or chop by hand). Return the chicken mixture to the skillet. Add the cream cheese, sour cream, and ranch dressing seasoning to the skillet and stir over medium-low heat, until the cream cheese is melted and the mixture is well combined. Turn off heat.

3. Pour the buffalo sauce into the skillet and drizzle in the honey. Stir in about three-quarters of the mozzarella and cheddar, and mix. Spread evenly in a 9 x 13-inch baking dish. Sprinkle the remaining cheeses evenly across the top.

4. Bake for 25 minutes. Serve hot, with the celery sticks and crackers.

IN A DASH: To save time, replace chicken with a pre-cooked, store-bought rotisserie chicken, removing skin and bones. Sprinkle with salt, black pepper, and garlic powder. Wait to add the chicken until Step 2.

BEER AND CHEESE FONDUE

MAKES 6 TO 8 SERVINGS

I'm bringin' back the fondue party! It's a great way to include guests who can't cook. You provide the meat (grilled steak, chicken, shrimp, or pork) and fondue with some Easy Roasted Veggies (185). Your guests can bring crudités or a fresh-baked bread for the savory . . . or fresh strawberries and brownies for the Chocolate Fondue (255).

¼ cup (½ stick) salted butter

2 garlic cloves, minced

Pinch of salt

2 T all-purpose flour or cornstarch

2 cups golden lager beer, such as Coors Banquet

1 tsp spicy brown mustard

1 tsp Worcestershire sauce

2 cups (16 ounces) freshly shredded sharp cheddar

1 cup (8 ounces) freshly shredded Swiss, Gruyère, or other semi-firm white cheese

2 ounces (¼ block) cream cheese, softened

⅛ teaspoon cayenne pepper

1. In a medium saucepan or pot, melt the butter over medium-low heat. Add the garlic and cook until fragrant, about 1 minute. Add a pinch of salt. Sprinkle in the flour and whisk until smooth. Gradually pour in the beer and whisk to thicken. Reduce the heat to low and add the mustard and Worcestershire sauce. Whisk continuously until the sauce is bubbling and thickened.

2. Add the cheddar, Swiss, and cream cheese, and whisk until the cheeses are melted. Season with cayenne. Serve in a fondue pot over a warmer.

Can be stored in an airtight container for 1 week. Ya may need to whisk in a splash of cream and garlic powder to bring the fondue back to life. Use the leftover fondue for broccoli cheese soup, au gratin potatoes, or pasta.

GREEN OLIVE SPREAD

MAKES 4 SERVINGS

One time, I had company coming over and I didn't have a thing to serve them. Broke and with no time to run to the store, I whipped up this little appetizer with what I had in the kitchen. The result was delicious. Serve it on crackers or sourdough toast.

3 ounces cream cheese, softened

⅓ cup mayonnaise

⅓ cup grated Parmesan

½ tsp garlic powder

½ tsp freshly ground black pepper

A few dashes cayenne pepper (optional)

1 cup (8 ounces) freshly shredded sharp Vermont white cheddar

⅓ cup drained and chopped pimento-stuffed green olives

Crackers and/or baguette slices, for serving

1. In a microwave-safe mixing bowl, heat the cream cheese 20 to 30 seconds, until it is easy to stir.

2. Mix in the mayo, Parmesan, garlic powder, black pepper, and cayenne until combined. Fold in the cheddar and then the olives.

3. The dip tastes best if chilled an hour before serving, but go ahead and dig in if you can't stand it.

Cover with plastic wrap and store in fridge for up to 6 days.

S
P

STUFFED ANGEL EGGS

MAKES 6 SERVINGS

I hate to call these "deviled eggs" because I don't associate with the devil. I refuse to eat these at covered dish functions because some people let their kitty cats walk across their countertops or they have a bad habit of licking their fingers while they're spooning in the filling. Gross. To fill the eggs I highly recommend using a piping gun or bag with a large star tip so that yours look prettier than everybody else's.

6 large eggs

¼ cup mayonnaise

2 to 3 T dill relish, drained

1 heaping tsp yellow mustard

Salt, to taste

Freshly ground black pepper, to taste

Smoked paprika, for garnish

Sliced pimento-stuffed olives, for garnish (optional)

1. Place the eggs in a medium saucepan or pot, and add enough water to cover by an inch. Bring to a rolling boil over high heat. Immediately turn off the heat, cover tightly, and let stand for 11 minutes (set a timer). Drain and cover with ice water.

2. To make 'em peel pretty, crack the top and bottom of the egg on your countertop, and lightly roll the egg along its center to loosen the shell. Rinse the peeled eggs and pat dry with paper towels.

3. Slice the eggs in half lengthwise. Carefully scoop the yolks into a small mixing bowl. Place the whites on your retro deviled egg dish. Smoosh the yolks with a fork or electric mixer until there are no large lumps. Add the mayonnaise, relish, and mustard, and season with salt and black pepper.

4. Put the yolk filling into a piping gun or bag with one of those fancy star tips, and fill your eggs. Garnish with smoked paprika and sliced olives (optional). Don't forget your relish tray in the center.

HOW TO MAKE ANGEL EGG SALAD

Just chop up the hard-boiled eggs and mix them in a bowl with the mayonnaise, relish, and mustard, and season with salt and pepper. You may want to add a tad more mayonnaise and fresh dill, if desired.

GETCHYO' MAN SCOTCH EGGS

MAKES 6 SERVINGS

I crave these on the regular. Mrs. Kathy Romersa taught me how to make them; she's a Tennessee debutante and a fabulous cook! Serve them hot as a party appetizer or with an arugula salad for a hang-over brunch.

SCOTCH EGGS

7 large eggs, divided

1 (5-ounce) bag pork rinds

⅓ cup breadcrumbs

1 tsp dried thyme leaves, rubbed between your fingertips to crush slightly

1 tsp garlic powder

½ tsp coarsely ground black pepper

½ tsp smoked paprika

¼ tsp cayenne pepper

4 tsp Dijon mustard

1 pound spicy pork, turkey, or venison sausage

Vegetable oil, for deep-frying, if needed

REMOULADE SAUCE

2 T mayonnaise

1 T ketchup

1 T Dijon mustard

½ tsp prepared horseradish

1. **SOFT-BOIL THE EGGS:** Place 6 eggs in a medium saucepan or pot and add enough water to cover by 1 inch. Bring to a rolling boil over high heat. Turn off the heat, cover tightly, and let stand for 6 to 7 minutes. Transfer to ice water.

2. To peel the soft-boiled eggs, carefully crack the top and bottom shell on your counter and lightly roll the egg on its center to break the shell. Remove the shell, rinse, and place the peeled eggs on a paper towel.

3. Pulse the pork rinds in a food processor until they are the texture of coarse breadcrumbs. Or you can make a small tear in the bag, cover the bag with a dish towel, and pound the shit out of them with a meat mallet until the rinds are powdered. Transfer to a medium bowl. Mix in the breadcrumbs, thyme, garlic powder, black pepper, paprika, and cayenne.

4. Whisk the remaining egg and the mustard in a separate small bowl.

5. Divide the sausage into 6 equal portions. Flatten each portion into a patty. Place an egg on a patty and mold the sausage around the egg to cover it completely. Pinch off the excess. You should have enough sausage leftover to make a small patty for you to cook and eat—chef's treat!

6. Roll each egg in the breadcrumb mixture to coat lightly. Then dip each egg into the mustard mixture and roll again in the breadcrumb mixture to coat well. Don't be afraid to pat the eggs into shape to make them pretty.

7. **FOR AN AIR FRYER:** Spray the basket with oil and preheat the air fryer to 400°F for 10 minutes. Quickly add the eggs to the basket, spacing them out, and fry for 6 to 7 minutes on each side.

FOR THE STOVETOP: Pour enough oil into a large saucepan or pot to come about 2 inches up the sides, and heat over high heat until the oil reads 350°F on a deep-frying thermometer. Carefully add the eggs to the oil and deep-fry, turning occasionally, until golden brown, about 5 minutes. Transfer the eggs to paper towels to cool slightly before serving.

8. **MAKE THE REMOULADE SAUCE:** Mix the mayonnaise, ketchup, mustard, and horseradish in a small bowl. Chill.

9. To serve, cut each egg in half and serve on a small plate. Drizzle the remoulade on top and serve immediately.

CHEF'S NOTE

If you'd like to make this even more keto-friendly, use almond flour in place of the breadcrumbs.

PIZZA DIP, IF YOU MUST

MAKES 10 TO 12 SERVINGS

I don't know what possesses people to put a layer of cream cheese without seasoning it on the bottom of a dip. Everybody winds up eating the topping and leaving the cream cheese behind. Looks trashy. Make it this way, Shoog. I use half turkey pepperoni so it's not swimming in grease.

16 ounces (2 blocks) cream cheese, softened

2 T pizza seasoning, preferably Flavor God (see Chef's Note)

5 ounces sliced pepperoni, cut in semicircles, divided

5 ounces sliced turkey pepperoni, cut in semicircles, divided

2 cups shredded low-moisture mozzarella, divided

½ cup grated Parmesan-Romano cheese blend

1 approximately (14-ounce) jar pizza sauce

Corn chip scoops, baguette slices, and/or celery sticks, for serving

1. Preheat the oven to 350°F. In a medium microwave-safe mixing bowl, heat the cream cheese 20 to 30 seconds, until it is easy to stir.

2. Mix the pizza seasoning into the cream cheese. Stir in about three-quarters of the regular and turkey pepperoni, and reserve the remaining pepperoni for the topping. Mix in 1 cup of the mozzarella and the Parmesan-Romano cheeses.

3. Spread the cheese mixture in the bottom of a 9 x 13-inch baking dish. Spread the pizza sauce on top and sprinkle with the remaining cup of mozzarella and reserved pepperoni. Make it pretty.

4. Bake uncovered for 25 minutes. (If you're feelin' extra, broil the dip for 3 to 4 minutes until the mozzarella is golden brown.) Serve hot, with the chips, baguette slices, or celery sticks.

CHEF'S NOTE

Substitute Flavor God's pizza seasoning with 1 tablespoon dry ranch seasoning mix, 1 teaspoon Italian seasoning, and 1 teaspoon garlic powder.

CROCK-POT COCKTAIL MEATBALLS

MAKES 10 TO 12 SERVINGS

For the busy host or hostess with the mostest . . . dump it all in the Crock-Pot and go do rockstar things.

1 (15-ounce) can tomato sauce (or crushed tomatoes)

1 (18-ounce) bottle Sweet Baby Ray's barbecue sauce

2 T white vinegar

2 T spicy brown mustard or yellow mustard

1 tsp sugar (or ½ packet of stevia)

1 (2-pound) bag frozen homestyle meatballs

1. Whisk the tomato sauce, barbecue sauce, white vinegar, mustard, and sugar in the base of your Crock-Pot. Add the meatballs, and submerge them in the sauce.

2. Cover and cook on high for 4 hours. Serve hot, with cocktail toothpicks. We're not animals.

CHEF'S NOTE

To make these keto or low-sugar friendly, just substitute a sugar-free barbecue sauce. No one will know.

LOW
HIGH
OFF
RIVAL

SPICED CANDIED PECANS

MAKES 2 CUPS

An easy, fancy appetizer for your "chatta-hoocherie" board. Sprinkle 'em on a salad or put 'em on your Christmas cookie giveaway trays. You'll want to make multiple batches of these, but only cook one batch at a time so you don't overcrowd the skillet. Have all the ingredients measured and ready to go before you start. This'll go fast!

1 tsp salt

½ tsp cayenne pepper

½ tsp ground cumin

½ tsp ground cinnamon

1 T granulated sugar

¼ heaping cup packed light brown sugar

1 T water

2 cups pecan halves

¼ cup (½ stick) salted butter

1. Line a cookie sheet with parchment paper. In a small bowl, whisk the salt, cayenne, cumin, and cinnamon. Set the seasoning mixture near the stove. In a separate small bowl add the granulated sugar and brown sugar, and set the bowl near the stove. Add the water to a tiny dish and place that near the stove too.

2. Heat a large heavy skillet (preferably cast iron, wide enough to hold the pecans in mostly a single layer) over medium heat. Toast the pecans, stirring occasionally, until they become fragrant, 2 to 3 minutes. Add the butter and cook, stirring often, until the pecans are coated in melted butter. Sprinkle with the seasoning mixture. Add the sugars and sprinkle with water. Quickly stir until the sugars are melted and the pecans are coated. Remove from the heat immediately and spread on the parchment-lined cookie sheet.

3. Allow the pecans to cool and transfer to an airtight container. Store at room temperature for up to 3 weeks or freeze for 3 months.

LOW COUNTRY BUTTER SHRIMP

MAKES 6 TO 8 SERVINGS

Don't use shrimpy shrimp. Get the big boys. This is Mother's recipe. Serve it with Beer Cheese Bread (80) to sop up the butter sauce. You're dang welcome.

1 cup (2 sticks) salted butter

⅔ cup olive oil

1 T paprika

1 T freshly ground black pepper

1 tsp fresh lemon juice

2 garlic cloves, minced

2 tsp crushed dried rosemary

½ tsp dried basil

½ tsp dried oregano

½ tsp salt

½ tsp cayenne pepper

4 whole bay leaves

2 pounds jumbo (21–25 count) raw shrimp, with heads removed, unpeeled

1. In a large saucepan or pot, heat the butter and oil over medium heat until the butter is melted. Add the paprika, black pepper, lemon juice, garlic, rosemary, basil, oregano, salt, cayenne, and bay leaves, and stir until the sauce boils. Simmer for approximately 7 to 8 minutes, stirring frequently. Remove the sauce from heat and let it stand for 30 minutes at room temperature.

2. Preheat the oven to 450°F. Add the shrimp to the herb butter and mix until the shrimp are coated. Return the pot to the burner and cook the shrimp, about 5 minutes over medium heat until they turn pink. Pour into 9 x 13-inch baking dish and bake for 8 to 10 minutes. Remove the bay leaves, and serve with beer bread. Peel the shrimp and eat!

Soups and Breads

RICH CHICKEN STOCK
RICH BEEF STOCK
RICH HAM STOCK
FROM-SCRATCH CREAM OF CHICKEN SOUP
FROM-SCRATCH CREAM OF MUSHROOM SOUP
BUTTERMILK CORNBREAD
CATHEAD BISCUITS
GARLIC CHEDDAR BUTTER BISCUITS
SOUR CREAM MINI MUFFINS
CINNAMON APPLE BEER BREAD
BEER CHEESE BREAD
BLUEBERRY BISCUITS WITH LEMON-CREAM GLAZE

RICH CHICKEN STOCK

MAKES ABOUT 2 QUARTS

Broth is Jim Parsons. *Stock* is Jason Momoa . . .

Basically, clean out your refrigerator. That celery that's about to go bad (leaves included), dry baby carrots, leftover onion . . . put it all in there. Every time you have a rotisserie or bone-in chicken, freeze the carcass (bones and trimmings, neckbones, giblets, etc.) to make homemade stock. Do *not* waste a thing or I will come after you.

1 small hen (2 to 4 pounds) cut into pieces, or 3 pounds chicken wings and leg quarters, or the carcass from a rotisserie (skin, bones, and wings included)

1 large yellow onion, coarsely chopped

2 to 3 large celery ribs, with leaves, coarsely chopped (1 to 1 ½ cups)

4 medium carrots, coarsely chopped

2 tsp whole black peppercorns

2 bay leaves

1 tsp sugar

2 quarts store-bought chicken stock

½ cup dry white wine, such as Chardonnay (optional)

Salt, to taste

1. Put the chicken in a tall pot or large Dutch oven with the onion, celery, carrots, peppercorns, bay leaves, and sugar. Pour in the stock and wine, if using, and add enough water to cover the chicken by an inch. Bring to a boil over medium-high heat, uncovered, then reduce heat to low and simmer 8 hours, covered. Salt to taste.

2. When stock is cool, remove the carcass and strain the veggie pieces over the stock pot with a cheesecloth or a mesh strainer. Squeeze or mush the veggies down with a large spoon to render all of that yummy liquid into the stock pot. Transfer to quart freezer bags or covered containers. (If you wish, remove the meat from the chicken bones and add it to the stock. This way you will have cooked chicken for your soup.)

The stock can be refrigerated for up to 3 days or frozen for up to 6 months.

IN A DASH: For a quicker stock, bring everything to a boil, then reduce to a strong simmer. Leave uncovered or partially covered, and let it go for 2 hours, instead of 8. Add water or store-bought stock if needed. You'll get a solid, flavorful stock—just lighter and less gelatin-rich than the long game. Still way better than anything straight from a box.

RICH BEEF STOCK

MAKES 2 TO 3 QUARTS

This is how I get rockstar flavor on a rockstar schedule. Don't overthink this one. The ingredient amounts don't have to be exact. Clean out your fridge and freezer! You likely have most of these ingredients on hand. You'll need some cheesecloth or a mesh strainer.

1 to 2 leftover ribeye or beef bones and trimmings (see Chef's Note)

1 yellow onion, cut into chunks

3 large celery ribs, roughly chopped (1 ½ cups)

3 medium carrots, coarsely chopped

2 ounces tomato paste (see Chef's Note)

1 heaping T brown sugar

Fresh or dried thyme

2 tsp whole black peppercorns

1 quart store-bought beef stock

½ cup dry red wine such as Cabernet or Merlot

Salt, to taste

1. Put the beef bones and trimmings in a tall pot or large Dutch oven, and add the onion, celery, carrots, tomato paste, brown sugar, thyme, peppercorns, stock, and wine.

2. Add enough water to fully submerge the contents by two inches. Bring to a rapid boil, then reduce the heat to low. Cover or partially cover and simmer for 8 hours. Salt to taste.

3. Allow the stock to cool, then remove and strain the veggies over the stock pot with a cheesecloth or a mesh strainer. Squeeze or mush down the veggies with a large spoon to render all of that yummy liquid into the stock pot. Discard bones and strain any meat and vegetable pieces. Store the stock in quart freezer bags or covered containers and freeze flat for up to 6 months.

CHEF'S NOTE

If you didn't save your steak bones and trimmings, ask your butcher for some neck bones, veal shanks, oxtail, or some affordable beef scraps on the bone. You'll need to coat these with some oil and roast at 425°F until brown, 45 to 60 minutes. Flip once halfway through. You're lookin' for deep brown, not burnt. Think "Sara Evans tan," not "Florida tourist red."

If I don't have tomato paste on hand I use Bloody Mary mix. About 1 ½ cups Bloody Mary mix, V8 juice, or similar tomato juice will do for a batch this size.

Use that bunch of herbs that's going bad in your crisper. Thyme and parsley are great. If using dried thyme, just use 1 to 2 teaspoons, crushed. Green bell pepper works well too.

RICH HAM STOCK

MAKES 4 CUPS

I discovered how to stretch my ham drippings and make 3 to 4 quarts of this stock from only one left-over ham. Jackpot! Use this in place of water when cooking down your favorite vegetables, like beans, peas, or collards. Don't have a ham? See Chef's Note.

1 T ham base, such as Better Than Bouillon

1 (6-ounce) can pineapple juice

½ tsp instant coffee

1 cup ham drippings, plus some ham trimmings with fat and skin (see Chef's Note)

2 cups water

1. Add the ham base, pineapple juice, instant coffee, ham drippings, ham trimmings, and water to a medium saucepan or pot, and bring to a boil over medium-high heat. Cover, reduce heat, and simmer for 20 minutes, or until most of the fat and flavor has rendered from the trimmings.

2. When the stock is cool, use a large strainer to remove the trimmings. Transfer to quart freezer bags or covered containers.

The stock can be refrigerated for up to 3 days or frozen for up to 6 months.

CHEF'S NOTE

Make sure your ham trimmings are predominantly ham skin with fat. This will render more flavor. If you don't have a ham, substitute 2 tablespoons bacon grease, 1 tablespoon brown sugar, 1 cup water, and 1 more teaspoon ham base or ½ packet Goya Ham Flavored Concentrate.

FROM-SCRATCH CREAM OF CHICKEN SOUP

MAKES 4 CUPS

Even if you're the busiest person in the world, you have time to make "cream of" soups. They taste so much better than the canned kind (gag a maggot). When I showed y'all how to make cream of chicken on TikTok, the video went viral—and for good reason! I freeze this in 1 1/4-cup portions to use in all my casseroles 'n' such.

2 T salted butter

2 T rendered chicken fat (see Chef's Note)

½ large white or yellow onion, chopped

2 large celery ribs, chopped (1 cup)

⅓ cup cooked and chopped chicken, seasoned with salt, pepper, and celery salt, to taste

¼ tsp celery salt

½ tsp garlic powder

⅛ tsp white pepper

3 T all-purpose flour

1 cup Rich Chicken Stock (64) or store-bought stock

2 ½ cups half-and-half

Salt, to taste

Freshly ground black pepper, to taste

1. In a large nonstick skillet, melt the butter and chicken fat over medium heat. Add the onion, celery, chicken, celery salt, garlic powder, and white pepper. Cook until the vegetables are tender, about 3 minutes. Sprinkle in the flour and stir until the flour turns pale beige, about 2 minutes.

2. Whisk in the stock, then the half-and-half. Bring to a simmer and reduce the heat to low. Simmer until thickened, about 2 to 3 minutes. Season with salt and black pepper to taste. Serve hot, or let cool and put in covered containers.

The soup can be cooled and refrigerated in covered containers or quart freezer bags for up to 3 days or frozen for up to 3 months.

IN A DASH: To save time on cooking chicken from scratch, you can always sub in a rotisserie chicken.

CHEF'S NOTE

To render chicken fat, collect the fat drippings whenever you roast or air fry chicken thighs (well-seasoned, with or without bone and skin) and pour them into a clean glass container with an airtight lid. The fat will keep for 2 weeks in the fridge or up to 6 months in the freezer (the salt from the seasoning helps to preserve it).

FROM-SCRATCH CREAM OF MUSHROOM SOUP

MAKES 4 CUPS

As God is my witness, Scarlett, you'll never buy canned cream of mushroom soup again. Serve this soup with a sandwich or as a fancy bisque. It's that good. Freezes well. Great in a casserole. You may need to fix it in two batches depending on the size of your skillet. Overcrowding your pan will render too much water from the vegetables.

2 T rendered beef fat

2 T salted butter, more as needed

1 large yellow onion, chopped

1 celery rib, chopped (½ cup)

¼ tsp celery salt

1 pound cremini, baby bella, or stemmed shiitake mushrooms, finely chopped

1 garlic clove, minced

½ tsp dried thyme, crushed between your fingertips

3 T all-purpose flour

2 cups Rich Beef Stock (65) or store-bought stock

1 cup half-and-half or heavy cream

2 T dry sherry, dry Marsala, or Madeira wine

Salt, to taste

Freshly ground black pepper, to taste

1. In a large, deep skillet, melt the beef fat and butter over medium heat. Add the onion, celery, and celery salt, and cook, stirring occasionally, until the veggies begin to soften, about 4 minutes. Add the mushrooms, garlic, and thyme. Cook, stirring often, until the mushrooms begin to brown, about 8 minutes. Sprinkle in the flour and stir well until the flour turns pale beige, about 2 minutes.

2. Gradually add the beef stock and half-and-half, and whisk until smooth. Simmer to thicken, about 3 minutes, and reduce heat to low. Add your sherry. Season with salt and black pepper to taste. Serve hot as a soup, or let cool and transfer to covered containers or quart freezer bags.

The soup can be refrigerated for up to 3 days or frozen for up to 3 months.

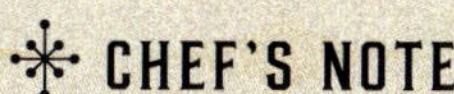

CHEF'S NOTE

Increase the sherry or wine to 1/4 cup if serving as a soup or bisque.

BUTTERMILK CORNBREAD

MAKES 8 SERVINGS

Don't come at me for putting a little sugar in my cornbread. I like mine moist and cakey. If you're making dressing, reduce the sugar by half.

¼ cup lard or vegetable shortening

1 cup white self-rising cornmeal mix, preferably White Lily

¾ cup self-rising flour, preferably White Lily

2 T sugar

½ tsp salt

1 cup buttermilk, preferably full fat

½ cup neutral oil, such as avocado or canola

2 large eggs

1 cup sour cream

1. Preheat the oven to 375°F. Put the lard or vegetable shortening in a heavy 10-inch skillet (preferably cast iron) or metal cake pan, and pop it in the oven during preheating. This should time out perfectly as you make your batter.

2. Whisk the cornmeal mix, self-rising flour, sugar, and salt in a medium bowl. Add the buttermilk, oil, eggs, and sour cream, and stir until just combined. Do not overstir.

3. Quickly pour the batter into the hot skillet, and bake for 20 to 25 minutes. Slice and serve warm with honey butter.

CATHEAD BISCUITS

MAKES 6 BISCUITS

Grab your 8-inch cast iron skillet. I had a ball making these on one of the last episodes of *The Rachael Ray Show*. I'm fixin' to give you the secrets to good, fluffy biscuits.

¼ cup lard

2 cups self-rising flour, preferably White Lily, plus more for shaping (see Chef's Note)

1 tsp baking soda

½ tsp salt

¼ cup (½ stick) salted butter, frozen

1 cup buttermilk, preferably full fat, more as needed

4 T (½ stick) salted butter, melted

1. Preheat the oven to 450°F. Place the lard in an 8-inch cast iron skillet (preferred) or metal cake pan (if you must), and pop it in the oven during preheating.

2. Sift the self-rising flour, baking soda, and salt into a medium bowl. Using the large holes on a box grater, grate your frozen butter right into the flour mixture. Don't leave any butter behind in the grater. Quickly toss the mixture together with your hands to distribute the butter evenly. Loosely stir in the buttermilk to moisten the flour (add a little more buttermilk if the dough seems dry). Do not overmix the dough.

3. Quickly remove the hot skillet with the lard from the oven and put it on a trivet near your work area. Flour your hands and scoop up about ⅓ cup of the dough. Toss it back and forth between your floured palms to shape into a rough biscuit (it only takes one or two tosses). Place the biscuit in the skillet and flip it over so the lard-coated top faces up. Repeat, making 6 biscuits total, placing the biscuits in a circle around the edge of the skillet and one in the center (the biscuits should touch each other). Pour the melted butter over the biscuits.

4. Bake for about 17 minutes, or until the biscuits are risen and golden brown. Serve warm. You can reheat these the same day, and they'll taste fresh. Wrap a biscuit in a damp paper towel and microwave for 10 seconds.

CHEF'S NOTE

If you're not using White Lily, double sift your flour into a separate bowl. (Do this in 2 separate bowls so you don't pack it down). Measure your 2 cups from that. And don't fret if you don't have frozen butter on hand. Grate it with your cheese grater onto a plate, and pop it into the freezer for 10 minutes to chill.

GARLIC CHEDDAR BUTTER BISCUITS

MAKES 9 BISCUITS

Pull UP, Red Lobster . . . these biscuits just stole yo' man.

¾ cup unsalted butter (1 ½ sticks), cut into tablespoons

2 tsp garlic powder, divided

2 ½ cups all-purpose flour

4 T baking powder

2 tsp sugar

½ tsp salt

1 cup buttermilk, preferably full fat

1 cup half-and-half

1 ½ cups freshly shredded sharp cheddar

Dried parsley, for the topping

1. Preheat the oven to 450°F. Melt the butter in the oven in a square 9 x 9-inch baking dish while oven preheats. Remove the butter when it is melted but not brown, and whisk in 1 teaspoon of garlic powder. Reserve 2 tablespoons of the garlic butter in a small bowl for the topping. Leave the remaining garlic butter in the baking dish.

2. In a mixing bowl, whisk the remaining garlic powder, flour, baking powder, sugar, and salt. Pour the buttermilk and half-and-half into the flour mixture and stir just until moistened—it can still be a little lumpy. Fold in the cheese. Pour the batter over the melted butter in the baking dish, and spread it evenly to the edges with your spoon. Using a dinner knife, cut the batter into 9 equal squares so the butter will travel everywhere. Pour the reserved garlic butter evenly over the batter. Sprinkle with dried parsley.

3. Bake until the biscuits are golden brown, about 25 to 28 minutes (reduce bake time by 5 to 10 minutes if using a metal baking pan). Let sit for 5 minutes and serve warm. You can reheat these the same day, and they'll taste fresh. Wrap a biscuit in a damp paper towel and microwave for 10 seconds.

SOUR CREAM MINI MUFFINS

MAKES 1 DOZEN

One bite and God visits Earth. These savory little angel nuggets pair with *any* meal: roasts, steaks, soups, chilis, and more. Try 'em with Pimento Cheese (41), Crock-Pot Apple Butter (208), or cane syrup.

Shortening, for greasing the pan

1 cup self-rising flour, preferably White Lily

¼ tsp salt

1 tsp sugar

½ cup (1 stick) salted butter, melted

1 heaping cup sour cream

1. Preheat the oven to 375°F. Liberally grease a 12-cup mini muffin pan with shortening. You will need to use a mini muffin tin for this recipe to help hold the muffins' shape.

2. Whisk the self-rising flour, salt, and sugar in a medium mixing bowl. Use a tablespoon to fold in the melted butter and sour cream. Do not over-mix. Pile 2 silver teaspoonfuls of dough into each cup. The dough mounds should sit about an inch above the rim. Or use a teaspoon to scrape the dough from the mixing spoon into each cup.

3. Bake for about 18 minutes. Serve immediately. You can reheat these the same day, and they'll taste fresh. Wrap a few muffins in a damp paper towel and microwave for 10 seconds.

CINNAMON APPLE BEER BREAD

MAKES 1 LOAF, 8 TO 10 SLICES

I recently took this to the Opry, and it was a hit backstage. When I perform there, I always take something convenient for me to make that I know will get eaten. This bread makes your house smell like a Bath & Body Works.

BATTER

3 cups self-rising flour, preferably White Lily

3 T granulated sugar

1 tsp ground cinnamon

1 ½ tsp salt

1 (12-ounce) bottle hard cider, such as Angry Orchard (see Chef's Note)

APPLE TOPPING

1 medium apple, peeled, cored and sliced thin

3 T brown sugar

½ tsp ground cinnamon

BROWN SUGAR CINNAMON LAYER

½ cup packed brown sugar

¼ cup (½ stick) salted butter, melted

1 tsp ground cinnamon

1 tsp vanilla extract

BUTTER TOPPING

½ cup (1 stick) salted butter, melted

1. Preheat the oven to 350°F. Grease your grandma's 9 x 5-inch loaf pan and set aside.

2. **Make the batter:** Whisk the self-rising flour, sugar, cinnamon, and salt in a large mixing bowl. Add the cider and stir just until combined. Do not overmix.

3. **Make the apple topping:** In a separate bowl, toss the apple with the brown sugar and cinnamon. Set aside. (Eat a few slices, you won't use it all.)

4. **Make the brown sugar cinnamon layer:** In a small bowl, stir to combine the brown sugar, ¼ cup of melted butter, cinnamon, and vanilla.

5. Pour half the bread batter into the pan. Dollop with the brown sugar mixture. Pour on the remaining batter and top it with ½ cup of melted butter (I slide a knife down the sides of the pan to let the butter run down). Do not stir or poke the batter. Place the apple slices on top. Sprinkle with more brown sugar and cinnamon, if desired, and bake.

6. Bake until the bread is risen and golden brown, about 50 minutes. Let cool for 5 minutes, then remove from the pan and slice to serve warm. To reheat, put a slice on a small plate with some butter and microwave for 10 to 20 seconds.

CHEF'S NOTE

This recipe will not work with an apple-flavored malt beverage. Stick to Angry Orchard, Strongbow, or other legit fermented apple juice.

BEER CHEESE BREAD

MAKES 1 LOAF, 8 SLICES

I don't fool with yeast. If I'm craving homemade bread, this one's my go-to. Quick and easy! Marry it with the Low Country Butter Shrimp (59), and they'll never get divorced. The Man Chili (143) too!

3 cups self-rising flour, preferably White Lily

1 ½ T sugar

1 ½ tsp salt

1 heaping cup freshly shredded sharp cheddar or pepper jack cheese

1 (12-ounce) bottle beer, such as Coors Banquet

½ cup (1 stick) salted butter, melted, divided

1. Preheat the oven to 350°F. Whisk the self-rising flour, sugar, and salt in a large mixing bowl. Add the cheese and toss to coat. Add the beer and stir just until combined. Do not overmix. Pour 4 tablespoons of the melted butter into a 9 x 5-inch loaf pan. Add your batter and top with remaining 4 tablespoons of melted butter. Pray over it.

2. Bake until the bread is risen and golden brown, about 50 minutes. Let cool for 5 to 10 minutes in the pan. Remove the bread from the pan to slice and serve warm. You can reheat this the same day or next day, and it'll taste fresh. Put a slice on a small plate with some butter and microwave for 10 to 20 seconds.

L'Echalote

BLUEBERRY BISCUITS WITH LEMON-CREAM GLAZE

✣ ✣

MAKES 9 BISCUITS

Blueberries and lemon go together like Conway and Loretta.

BLUEBERRY BISCUITS

10 T (5/8 cup) unsalted butter

1 heaping cup fresh or frozen blueberries

3 T granulated sugar, divided

2 ½ cups all-purpose flour, preferably White Lily

4 T baking powder

½ tsp salt

1 cup buttermilk, preferably full fat

1 cup half-and-half

LEMON-CREAM GLAZE

1 cup powdered sugar, divided, as needed

1 tsp finely grated lemon zest

2 T fresh lemon juice

3 T heavy cream, as needed

1. **Make the biscuits:** Preheat the oven to 450°F. Place the butter in a a 9 x 9-inch baking dish, and pop the dish in the oven during preheating. Remove when butter is melted but not brown.

2. In a small bowl, toss the blueberries with 2 tablespoons of sugar and set aside. Then, in a medium bowl, whisk the flour, baking powder, remaining tablespoon of sugar, and salt. Pour the buttermilk and half-and-half into the flour mixture and loosely stir, just until combined. Don't overmix. Carefully fold in the blueberries and their juices.

3. Pour the batter into the melted butter in the baking dish, and smooth to the edges with a dinner knife. Cut the batter into 9 equal squares to ensure the butter runs evenly into the cuts. Bake until golden brown, 28 to 30 minutes.

4. **Make the lemon-cream glaze:** Whisk ½ cup of the powdered sugar and the lemon zest and juice in a medium bowl (this stops the cream from curdling when it is added to the glaze). Add the remaining ½ cup powdered sugar and the cream. Whisk until smooth and pourable. If the glaze is too thick, add a little more cream. If it is too thin, add a little more powdered sugar. Pour the glaze over the warm biscuits and serve.

The biscuits can be cooled, covered, and refrigerated for up to 3 days. To reheat individual biscuits, microwave for 20 to 30 seconds.

Salads and Dressings

ORANGE MOUNTAIN SALAD

MAKES 10 TO 12 SERVINGS

In old society, a cold salad was served with every meal. These are some easy-to-make Dasher family favorites that'll add some color to your table. And for the love, serve it in vintage glass.

1 (24-ounce) container small curd cottage cheese

1 (20-ounce) can crushed pineapple, drained

1 (6-ounce) package orange-flavored gelatin dessert

1 (8-ounce) container thawed whipped topping, such as Cool Whip

2 (11-ounce) cans mandarin oranges, drained

½ cup chopped pecans

1. Put the cottage cheese and pineapple in a large bowl. Sprinkle the gelatin mix evenly over the top, and mix well until the gelatin is moistened. Let stand 5 minutes. Fold in the whipped topping and then the oranges and pecans. Reserve a few oranges and some of the whipped topping for garnish.

2. Cover with plastic wrap and refrigerate until chilled and set, about 8 hours. Serve in sherbet glasses and top with whipped topping, and orange slices if you're fun.

The salad can be refrigerated for up to 3 days.

CHEF'S NOTE

Cut carbs and calories by using a sugar-free gelatin.

HOW TO MAKE STRAWBERRY FLUFF SALAD: If you'd rather have pink on your plate than orange, try a Strawberry Fluff. Omit the mandarin oranges and substitute strawberry-flavored gelatin for the orange-flavored. Garnish with fresh strawberries, if desired.

BROCCOLI SALAD

MAKES 10 SERVINGS

Here's another unhealthy way to eat your vegetables. This was a staple at ladies gatherings at my little country church. Raw veggies can make your tummy pooch, so blanch your broccoli, Linda. It's easier on the gut. Make a day ahead for best results, and use more bacon if desired.

DRESSING

1 cup mayonnaise

¼ cup sugar, more as needed

2 T cider vinegar

⅛ tsp garlic powder

Salt, to taste

Freshly ground black pepper, to taste

SALAD

2 large heads broccoli, cut into florets

Salt, to taste

Freshly ground black pepper, to taste

1 cup raisins

½ small red onion, chopped

½ cup chopped cashews

8 ounces (½ pound) bacon, cooked until crisp, chopped

1. **Make the dressing:** Whisk the mayonnaise, sugar, vinegar, and garlic powder in a large bowl until the sugar dissolves. Season with salt and black pepper, and more sugar, if desired.

2. **Make the salad:** Bring a large pot of salted water to a boil. Add the broccoli and cook just until it turns a brighter shade of green, about 1 ½ minutes. Drain, rinse under cold water, and drain again. Pat dry with paper towels. Coarsely chop the broccoli into small pieces.

3. Add the broccoli to the salad bowl and season it with salt and fresh cracked pepper. Add the raisins, onion, and cashews and mix well. Cover the salad and refrigerate for 4 hours or preferably overnight. Store bacon in an airtight container until ready to serve. Stir in the bacon, reserving some to sprinkle liberally on top, and serve cold.

This can be refrigerated for up to 3 days in an airtight container.

COOL CARROTS (AKA COPPER PENNIES)

MAKES 10 TO 12 SERVINGS

I crave these every spring and summer (think Easter 1962). They add some color to your plate and keep for five days in the fridge as a quick side to any meal. Don't use baby carrots; buy the adult sized.

2 pounds carrots, peeled and sliced into ½-inch coins

1 (10.75-ounce) can tomato soup

1 cup sugar

¾ cup white vinegar

½ cup olive oil

1 T yellow mustard

1 medium green bell pepper, seeded and chopped

½ large white onion, cut into thin half-moons

1. Bring a medium saucepan or pot of well-salted water to a boil over high heat. Add the carrots and cook until tender, about 10 to 12 minutes. Drain and transfer to a medium bowl.

2. In the same pot, whisk the tomato soup, sugar, vinegar, oil, and mustard. Add the green pepper and onions, and bring the mixture to a simmer over medium-high heat. Boil for 5 minutes.

3. Pour the tomato soup mixture over the carrots and stir. Let cool. Cover tightly and refrigerate for 1 day before serving. Serve cold.

The carrots can be refrigerated for up to 5 days in an airtight container.

IN A DASH: Swap canned carrots for fresh. Use approximately 4 (14.5-ounce) cans, drained. Skip to Step 2.

SOUTHERN CHICKEN SALAD

MAKES 8 SERVINGS

Grapes in chicken salad is like John Denver in country music . . . This chicken salad is at its best with Grandma's 14-Day Sweet Pickles (200); otherwise use a high-quality sweet pickle.

4 cups cooked chicken, chopped (white and dark meat from a rotisserie chicken)

1 to 2 large celery ribs, diced (⅔ cup)

1 (4-ounce) jar diced pimentos, drained

½ cup chopped sweet pickles

1 cup mayonnaise, as needed

1 tsp garlic powder

1 tsp salt

1 tsp freshly ground black pepper

¼ tsp cayenne pepper

2 to 3 hard-boiled eggs, chopped

½ cup toasted pecans, optional

In a large bowl, combine the chicken, celery, pimentos, and sweet pickles. Add the mayonnaise, garlic powder, salt, black pepper, and cayenne, and stir to combine. Add the eggs last so they stay pretty. Top with pecans, if using. Cover and refrigerate until ready to serve, up to 4 days.

CHEF'S NOTE

To make Sweet 'n' Spicy Chicken Salad, substitute candied jalapeños for the sweet pickles (I like Buc-ee's version). Discard as many seeds as possible.

CUCUMBER TOMATO SALAD

MAKES 10 TO 12 SERVINGS

I don't like raw tomatoes or cucumbers, but I luvvv this Southern classic. This was my first recipe to go viral. Use locally grown veggies if accessible, and store this in retro Tupperware like your grandma did.

¼ cup sugar

¼ cup olive oil

½ cup cider vinegar

2 T water

½ tsp salt

¼ tsp freshly ground black pepper

4 small cucumbers, peeled and cut into ¼-inch rounds

½ large Vidalia onion, cut into thin half-moons

1 large heirloom tomato, chopped into chunks

1. In a medium bowl, whisk the sugar, oil, vinegar, and water to dissolve the sugar. Whisk in the salt and pepper. Add the cucumber, onion, and tomato, and mix it all up.

2. Cover and refrigerate for at least 1 hour. This salad gets better as it sits! Let it stand at room temperature for 20 minutes before serving if the oil has solidified.

The salad can be refrigerated for up to 5 days in an airtight container. (though Nana kept hers all summer and just added more vegetables to it).

CHEF'S NOTE

To easily make this from memory, I just remember *quarter, quarter, half, splash*:

¼ cup sugar, ¼ cup oil, ½ cup vinegar, splash of water.

You know the rest . . .

PERFECT PASTA SALAD

MAKES 8 SERVINGS

Best pasta salad I've ever put in my mouth. The boys at *The Fowl Life* have been big supporters of my music. I'm not a product pusher, but their Crosshairs seasoning at the Provider Life is somethin' else ! It makes the dish. I've listed a substitute below.

1 pound elbow macaroni

1 T garlic salt

1 heaping cup mayonnaise

½ cup dill relish, drained

½ cup high-quality sweet pickles, preferably Grandma's 14-Day Sweet Pickles (200), chopped

¼ cup dill pickle juice

3 T Crosshairs seasoning (see Chef's Note), plus more for garnish

1 tsp yellow mustard

Salt, to taste

Freshly ground black pepper, to taste

1. Bring a large pot of water to a boil over high heat. Add the macaroni and garlic salt. Cook according to the package directions until the pasta is tender. Drain in a colander.

2. Mix the mayonnaise, dill relish, sweet pickles, dill pickle juice, Crosshairs seasoning, and mustard in a large bowl. Add the macaroni and stir to combine. Season with salt and black pepper. Cover and refrigerate for 1 hour. Sprinkle with more seasoning and serve.

The salad can be refrigerated for up to 7 days in an airtight container.

CHEF'S NOTE

Crosshairs seasoning is a dill-based rub with lemon pepper and garlic. You could substitute 1 teaspoon beef bouillon powder, 1 teaspoon garlic powder, 1 teaspoon nutritional yeast (optional), 1/2 teaspoon dried dill, 1/2 teaspoon salt, 1/2 teaspoon coarsely ground black pepper, and 1/2 teaspoon lemon pepper. You can buy Crosshairs directly from The Provider at theproviderlife.com.

PROPER POTATO SALAD

MAKES 10 TO 12 SERVINGS

In the South, the fastest way to get judged is to bring store-bought potato salad to a meal. This is the first dish I ever made by myself as a kid, so I have confidence you can do it too. Here's my grown-up recipe. Serve it warm or cold.

2 ½ pounds Yukon Gold potatoes, unpeeled, cut into 2-inch chunks

2 large eggs

⅔ cup mayonnaise, as needed

¼ cup sour cream

1 T yellow mustard

2 T white vinegar

1 tsp salt

1 tsp freshly ground black pepper

½ tsp garlic powder

½ cup minced white onion

½ cup high-quality sweet pickles, preferably Grandma's 14-Day Sweet Pickles (200), chopped

Smoked paprika, for garnish

Bacon crumbles, for garnish

1. Put the potatoes and eggs in a pot of well-salted water and cook over high heat. Simmer until the potatoes are just tender but not mushy, about 12 minutes. Transfer the eggs to a bowl of iced water to cool. Drain the potatoes, and peel and chop the eggs.

2. Mix the dressing now so you don't tear the potatoes all to hell. Whisk the mayonnaise, sour cream, mustard, vinegar, salt, pepper, and garlic powder in a large bowl to combine. Stir in the onion and sweet pickles. Fold in the potatoes and eggs. Season with more salt and cracked pepper if desired. Sprinkle with paprika to make it pretty. Serve warm or allow to cool; then cover and refrigerate to serve cold.

The salad can be refrigerated for up to 3 days in an airtight container. Top with crispy bacon if you're feeling ratchet.

EVELYN'S EDAMAME SALAD

MAKES 10 SERVINGS

This one's high-protein and Wilson approved (Wilson's my personal trainer). One of my rock 'n' roll girlfriends turned me onto this (Evyn Johnston—I call her Evelyn—she's a fabulous cook). Use lots of freshly ground pepper. Double the cranberries if you're feelin' skinny.

2 (10-ounce) bags frozen shelled edamame

3 T olive oil

8 ounces feta cheese, crumbled

1 ½ cups dried cranberries

3 T chopped fresh basil

1 packet stevia

Salt, to taste

Freshly ground black pepper, to taste

1. Boil or steam the edamame in the microwave until tender, cooking 1 minute longer than the package directions. Drain and rinse under cold water. Transfer to a large bowl.

2. Add the oil and toss well to coat. Add the feta, cranberries, and basil, sprinkle with the stevia, and toss again. Season with salt and plenty of black pepper.

3. Cover and refrigerate until ready to serve, at least 2 hours. This gets even better as it sits.

This salad can be refrigerated for 5 days in an airtight container.

BUSY GIRL BOW TIE SALAD

MAKES 10 SERVINGS

This is a good salad for a party or for meal prep. If you're looking for a heartier one-dish option, add a grilled protein or some garbanzo beans.

8 ounces bow tie pasta

1 (0.6-ounce) packet zesty Italian dressing mix

1 ½ T dry white wine or champagne (optional)

¼ cup red wine vinegar or cider vinegar

1 ½ T water

½ cup olive oil

1 (5-ounce) bag fresh baby spinach, tough stems removed

½ cup sun-dried tomatoes, julienned or chopped

1 small red onion, thinly sliced

½ cup feta cheese, crumbled

1. Cook the pasta in salted water according to package directions. Drain and rinse under cold water. Transfer to a pretty salad bowl. (If you don't plan to serve immediately, toss the pasta with a splash of oil to keep it from sticking.)

2. In a small lidded jar, add the packet of zesty Italian dressing mix, white wine, vinegar, water, and oil. Shake well.

3. When you're ready to serve, to the cooled pasta add the spinach, sun-dried tomatoes, red onion, and feta, and toss well. If you don't anticipate having many leftovers, add the dressing to the pasta mixture and toss. Otherwise, serve the salad with dressing on the side.

The salad can be covered and refrigerated for up to 3 days in an airtight container.

IN A DASH: I often flip this side dish into meal prep. I just pair it with a grilled protein and use a protein pasta instead. I keep everything in separate containers so the ingredients stay fresh. This is great to take on the go or to serve as a last-minute side during the week, Mama!

SEVEN-LAYER SALAD

MAKES 10 TO 12 SERVINGS

A foolproof Southern classic. This salad keeps crispy in the fridge for several days. Serve the dressing in a separate bowl so it doesn't wilt the salad.

DRESSING

1 cup mayonnaise

2 T sugar

2 T white vinegar

½ tsp garlic salt

SALAD

1 head iceberg lettuce, chopped into bite-size pieces

2 medium carrots, peeled and shredded (1 cup)

1 small red onion, chopped

4 cups frozen green peas, cooked and cooled

4 hard-boiled eggs, chopped

8 strips bacon, cooked until crisp, and chopped

2 cups freshly shredded sharp cheddar or Colby Jack cheese

1. **Make the dressing:** Whisk the mayonnaise, sugar, vinegar, and garlic salt together in a small bowl to dissolve the sugar. Cover tightly and chill. Just before serving, transfer to a pretty little serving bowl. We're not animals.

2. **Layer the salad:** In a large glass serving bowl or trifle dish, layer the lettuce along the bottom. Top with the carrots, onion, peas, eggs, bacon, and cheese, adding everything in layers. Cover with plastic wrap and refrigerate until ready to serve. Make sure the bacon is extra crispy so it doesn't get soggy.

3. Serve the salad chilled with the dressing on the side.

The salad can be refrigerated for up to 3 days in an airtight container.

SHRIMP AND TOMATO ASPIC

MAKES 10 TO 12 SERVINGS

I never touched this stuff as a kid, but these days I get a hankering for it. This dish is a beautiful, classy touch to any gathering. It's a great way to elevate your dinner party. If you don't like it, serve it to the guests you're hoping to run off sooner than later.

¼ cup water

2 envelopes plain powdered gelatin

2 (10.5-ounce) cans condensed tomato soup

6 ounces (¾ block) cream cheese, softened

1 cup mayonnaise

1 cup cooked shrimp, chopped

1 cup walnuts, chopped

⅔ cup celery, minced

⅔ cup yellow onion, minced

⅔ cup green bell pepper, seeded and minced

Oil, for the mold

Lettuce leaves, for serving 10 to 12 large, tail-on cocktail shrimp, for garnish

1. Pour water into a cup or ramekin. Sprinkle in the gelatin and set it aside for 5 to 10 minutes to soften.

2. Heat the undiluted tomato soup and cream cheese in a medium saucepan or pot over medium heat, whisking often, until the cheese has melted and the mixture is well combined. Reduce the heat to very low. Add the softened gelatin and whisk until the gelatin is completely melted. Pour the tomato mixture into a bowl. Add the mayonnaise and whisk until combined.

3. Refrigerate until the tomato mixture begins to thicken, about 1 ½ hours. Fold in the shrimp, walnuts, celery, onion, and bell pepper.

4. Lightly oil a 4-cup Jell-O or copper mold. Pour in the aspic. Refrigerate until chilled and set, about 4 hours. Invert to unmold the congealed salad onto a lettuce-lined silver platter. Garnish with more cocktail shrimp, if desired.

CHEF'S NOTE

If you don't have a mold, use a Bundt pan instead. Just be sure to cover with cling wrap before refrigerating.

STRAWBERRY PRETZEL SALAD

MAKES 12 TO 15 SERVINGS

When I was growing up in the '90s, my family served this every Christmas. I'll be eatin' it 'til Jesus comes back. This is best if prepared one day ahead.

CRUST

2 heaping cups pretzels (pretzel sticks work best), crushed

10 T (⅝ cup) butter, melted

¼ cup granulated sugar

FILLING

8 ounces (1 block) cream cheese, softened

1 ½ cups granulated sugar

1 tsp vanilla extract

1 ¼ cups heavy cream

2 T powdered sugar

TOPPING

1 (6-ounce) package strawberry gelatin dessert

1 ½ cups boiling water

1 pint frozen sliced strawberries with sugar, thawed but chilled

1. **Make the crust:** Preheat the oven to 350°F. Mix the pretzels, butter, and sugar in a large bowl. Press the mixture firmly and evenly into a 9 x 13-inch baking dish. Bake until it smells toasty, about 10 minutes. Let cool completely.

2. **Make the filling:** In a large bowl, using an electric mixer on medium speed, beat the cream cheese, granulated sugar, and vanilla until smooth. In a separate, chilled medium bowl, beat the heavy cream and powdered sugar on high speed until stiff. Fold the whipped cream into the cream cheese mixture. Spread the filling evenly onto the cooled crust, sealing it to the sides of the dish so the topping won't leak down. Refrigerate while making the topping.

3. **Make the topping:** In a separate bowl, whisk the gelatin and boiling water together to dissolve completely. Add the strawberries and their juices and stir. Set this bowl in the fridge to chill for 10 minutes, or until partially set.

4. Carefully pour the strawberry mixture over the cream cheese filling. Cover with plastic wrap and refrigerate until completely set, at least 12 hours or overnight.

HOSTESS NOTE

If you're feeling patriotic, sprinkle in some fresh blueberries at the beginning of step 4. God bless America.

WATERGATE SALAD

MAKES 8 TO 10 SERVINGS

This stuff is the color of 1950s wall paint. It's pistachio-pudding heaven and a fun way to use those sherbet glasses sitting in your china cabinet. Here's my version . . .

1 (20-ounce) can crushed pineapple, drained, juice reserved

1 (3.4-ounce) package pistachio instant pudding mix

½ cup pistachios, walnuts, or pecans, chopped

2 cups Better Than Whipped Cream (213) or thawed frozen whipped topping, like Cool Whip

1 heaping cup mini marshmallows

½ cup chocolate chips, semisweet or dark

Maraschino cherries, drained, for garnish

1. Reserve about one third of the juice from the pineapple and drain off the rest. Put the pineapple and juice in a large bowl. Sprinkle the pudding mix on top and mix well. Stir in the nuts. Fold in the whipped cream, marshmallows, and chocolate chips. Transfer to a pretty glass serving bowl.

2. Cover with plastic wrap and refrigerate until chilled and set, about 8 hours. Garnish with drained Maraschino cherries. Serve chilled.

The salad can be refrigerated for up to 3 days.

BALSAMIC VINAIGRETTE

MAKES ABOUT 3/4 CUP

For the love, Linda, don't buy that cheap mess at the store. Make your own! Toss this on your favorite salad, or use it as a marinade for chicken, salmon, and pork tenderloin.

¼ cup olive oil

¼ cup balsamic vinegar

2 T honey

1 T dry white wine or champagne (optional)

1 T Dijon mustard

2 T fresh lemon juice

1 T red onion, minced

1 tsp garlic powder

½ tsp salt

½ tsp freshly ground black pepper

Pour the oil, vinegar, honey, wine, mustard, lemon juice, onion, garlic powder, salt, and pepper in one of those pretty salad shakers or a Mason jar, and shake the shit out of it.

The dressing can be refrigerated for up to 1 week. Shake before using.

THOUSAND ISLAND DRESSING

MAKES ABOUT 1 CUP

Please don't tell people this is my recipe if you use lite mayonnaise to make it. I put this on wedge salads, burgers, dogs, sandwiches, and even French fries.

½ cup mayonnaise

¼ cup dill relish

Scant ¼ cup ketchup

3 T red onion, minced

2 T white vinegar

1 T sugar

Salt, to taste

Freshly ground black pepper, to taste

Water, as needed

Whisk the mayonnaise, dill relish, ketchup, onion, vinegar, and sugar to dissolve the sugar. Season with salt and pepper. Add a tiny splash of water to thin the dressing to a desired consistency.

This dressing can be covered and refrigerated for up to 4 days.

L'Echalote

Mains

GETCHYO' MAN BEEF ROAST
KEEP YO' MAN STUFFED PEPPERS
SISSY'S SHEPHERD'S PIE
SUND'Y HAM
POTATO CHIP PORK CHOPS
LOW COUNTRY BOIL
BISCUIT BLTS WITH PIMENTO CHEESE
ROCKSTAR CABBAGE
OVEN-FRIED CANE BUTTER CHICKEN
GETCHYO' MAN FRIED CHICKEN FINGERS
WHITE CHICKEN CHILI
VEGGIE CHILI
MAN CHILI
TULSA CHICKEN 'N' GRAVY
"MA, THE MEATLOAF!"
CHICKEN PIE
CHICKEN SCALLOP
FRIED CHICKEN LIVERS WITH PORT WINE SAUCE
FRIED CATFISH PO'BOYS
MAMA'S TOMATO PIE

GETCHYO' MAN BEEF ROAST

MAKES 6 TO 8 SERVINGS

Yankees call it pot roast; Southerners call it beef stew or beef roast. Some dare to cook this in a Crock-Pot (cringe). Quit that right now and try it the old-fashioned way! No dry, stringy meat with watery gravy here. If Zach Top or Scott Eastwood were coming over for supper, this is what I'd fix 'em.

ROAST

- 3 medium Yukon Gold potatoes, unpeeled, quartered
- ½ large yellow or Vidalia onion, sliced into thick half-moons
- 1 pound baby carrots
- 2 ½ tsp salt, divided
- 2 ½ tsp freshly ground black pepper, divided
- 2 tsp garlic powder, divided
- 1 (2 to 3-pound) well-marbled chuck roast or bone-in ribeye roast
- ¼ tsp cayenne pepper
- ⅓ cup all-purpose flour
- 2 T neutral oil, such as avocado or canola

GRAVY

- 2 T rendered steak fat, bacon grease, or salted butter
- ½ large yellow or Vidalia onion, finely chopped
- 2 garlic cloves, finely chopped
- 3 cups Rich Beef Stock (65) or store-bought stock
- ½ cup dry red wine or lager beer
- ½ tsp garlic powder
- ½ tsp freshly ground black pepper
- Salt, as needed

1. **Make the roast:** Preheat the oven to 275°F. Arrange potatoes, onion slices, and carrots around the edges of a large lidded roasting pan. (I put a couple onions and potatoes in the center of the pan—spaced out—to create a platform for my roast, but you don't have to.) Season vegetables with 1 tsp each of salt, black pepper, and garlic powder.

2. On a large plate, season the roast on each side with the remaining salt, pepper, garlic powder, and cayenne. Liberally rub the top, bottom, and sides with the flour. Shake off the excess flour onto the plate and reserve this for the gravy.

3. Heat the oil in a large, deep skillet (preferably nonstick) on medium heat. Add the roast and sear on one side for 5 to 7 minutes, or until the flour forms a

light brown crust. Flip over the roast and brown the other side, about 4 minutes more. Quickly sear the sides, and transfer the roast to the center of the roasting pan.

4. **Make the gravy:** In the same skillet, reduce heat to medium-low and melt whatever fat you're using. Cook the onion and garlic for 2 minutes. Add the plate of reserved seasoned flour (about 3 tablespoons), and whisk to incorporate it with the fat in the pan. Let it brown for 1 to 2 minutes. Gradually whisk in the stock, then the wine (or beer), and bring to a simmer. Season with garlic powder and black pepper. Taste for salt. Add more if desired. Pour the gravy over the roast and veggies.

5. Cover and bake for 3 ½ hours, until the roast is fork-tender. To serve, transfer the roast and vegetables to a platter with the gravy (use a gravy boat, if you're old-school). Serve over mashed potatoes, Proper Grits (187), or rice.

HOSTESS NOTE

Enjoy a roast for Sunday lunch and eat the leftovers over grits for Monday breakfast.

KEEP YO' MAN STUFFED PEPPERS

MAKES 4 SERVINGS

One of Hank Jr.'s favorite foods is stuffed peppers. I first made these with his daughter Hilary using meat from an elk he shot (ground beef or venison work well too!). This is one of my favorite weeknight meals, and it tastes even better the next day.

PEPPERS

1 T garlic salt

5 large bell peppers (green, yellow, orange, or red—preferably several colors)

½ cup uncooked white rice

2 T olive oil, plus more for the baking dish

1 medium yellow onion, chopped

¼ tsp celery salt

4 garlic cloves, finely chopped

¼ cup Rich Beef Stock (65) or store-bought stock

1 pound ground turkey (93% lean) or venison

1 (15-ounce) can petite diced tomatoes, undrained

1 (10 to 12-ounce) bag frozen riced cauliflower, cooked

Salt, to taste

Freshly ground black pepper, to taste

½ cup crumbled feta cheese, plus more for garnish

1 T dried cilantro, plus more for garnish

SOUTHWEST SEASONING

1 T chili powder

1 ½ tsp ground cumin

1 tsp garlic powder

1 tsp freshly ground black pepper

1 tsp sugar

½ tsp sweet paprika

¼ tsp cayenne

¼ tsp dried oregano

1. Preheat the oven to 350°F. Bring a large pot of water to a boil over high heat. Add the garlic salt. Meanwhile, slice the tops off the peppers and scoop out and discard the ribs and seeds to make pepper cups. Chop and reserve the excess flesh around the stems, and discard the stems. Boil the pepper cups in the seasoned water until they have a little bend to them, about 5 minutes. Use tongs to remove the peppers and let them drain upside down on paper towels.

2. Add a cup of the seasoned water to a small pot and bring to a rapid boil. Add the rice, cover tightly, and reduce the heat to low. Simmer for 20 minutes or until tender.

3. Meanwhile, make the Southwest Seasoning: Mix the chili powder, cumin, garlic powder,

black pepper, sugar, paprika, cayenne, and oregano together in a ramekin. Set aside.

4. Heat the oil in a large, deep skillet over medium heat. Add the onion, reserved chopped peppers and celery salt and cook until tender, about 4 minutes. Stir in the garlic and cook until fragrant, about 1 minute. Set the veggies aside in a bowl, and deglaze the pan with beef stock, loosening up any browned bits with your spoon.

5. Add the meat and Southwest Seasoning. Cook, stirring to break up the meat until browned, about 5 minutes. Stir in the can of tomatoes, sautéed vegetables, cooked rice, and cauliflower rice. Season with salt and black pepper. Gently stir in the feta cheese and cilantro.

6. Stuff the peppers with the mixture, and put them in a cast iron skillet or a 9 x 9-inch baking dish. Bake for 20 minutes. Garnish with more cilantro and serve hot.

IN A DASH: Substitute the Southwest Seasoning with a packet of taco seasoning. Do not dilute with water. Ground beef works great in this recipe too.

SISSY'S SHEPHERD'S PIE

MAKES 10 TO 12 SERVINGS

They served this to us in public school, and I gagged . . . until I had my sister Brittany's version. I sometimes divide the filling and topping between two deep-dish pie pans and freeze one for another meal. Just thaw overnight in the fridge before baking, or microwave on low until thawed.

POTATO TOPPING

2 pounds baking potatoes, such as russet or Yukon Gold, peeled and cut into 1-inch chunks

2 ounces (¼ block) cream cheese, softened

½ cup heavy cream or half-and-half

½ cup sour cream

¼ cup (½ stick) salted butter, melted

1 cup grated Parmesan or shredded sharp Vermont white cheddar

Salt, to taste

1 large egg, beaten

FILLING

1 T oil

1 ½ pounds ground chuck (80% lean)

½ medium yellow onion, chopped

2 cups baby carrots, sliced

2 garlic cloves, minced

5 T tomato paste

1 T Worcestershire sauce, preferably Bear & Burton's W Sauce

1 T soy sauce

1 tsp chili powder

1 tsp dried oregano

1 tsp dried thyme, crushed

1 (1.61-ounce) packet brown gravy mix, preferably Pioneer

2 ½ cups Rich Beef Stock (65) or store-bought stock

1 cup frozen sweet peas

Salt, to taste

Freshly ground black pepper, to taste

1. Preheat the oven to 400°F. Line a baking sheet with aluminum foil.

2. **Make the topping:** In a large pot of well-salted water, bring the potatoes to a boil. Reduce heat to medium and simmer until tender, about 20 minutes. Drain the potatoes. Put them through a ricer into a large bowl (or mash 'em any way you like, as long as there are no lumps). Add the cream cheese, heavy cream (or half-and-half), sour cream and butter and mix until combined. Stir in the Parmesan (or cheddar) and add salt to taste. Mix in the egg, and set aside.

3. Meanwhile, **make the filling:**

Heat the oil in a large skillet over medium-high heat. Add the ground chuck and cook until browned, stirring occasionally, about 8 minutes. Transfer the beef to a bowl, leaving the fat in the skillet.

4. Add the onion and carrots to the skillet and cook, stirring occasionally, until the carrots are almost tender, about 4 minutes. Stir in the garlic and cook until fragrant, about 1 minute. Add the tomato paste, Worcestershire sauce, soy sauce, chili powder, oregano, and thyme and stir well.

5. In a medium bowl, whisk the gravy mix and beef stock to dissolve the mix. Return the meat to the skillet with the vegetables; add the gravy mixture and bring to a simmer. Reduce the heat to medium-low and cover. Simmer until thickened, about 15 minutes. Stir in the peas. Season with salt and black pepper.

6. Spread the filling in a 15 x 10-inch baking pan. Add the potato topping, using a metal spatula to spread, making sure the potatoes touch the sides of the dish to keep the filling from boiling over. (I like to pipe the filling through a pastry gun with a large star tip. Pipe to the edges to cover completely.) Place the baking dish on the foil-lined baking sheet.

7. Bake until the topping is tinged with brown and the filling is bubbling, about 30 minutes. Transfer to a wire cooling rack and let stand for 15 minutes before serving.

SUND'Y HAM

MAKES 10 TO 12 SERVINGS

My parents took us to church every Sunday, and there was always fried chicken, roast, or ham for Sunday dinner (that's Southern for "lunch"). You can make several meals off one ham. Use your leftover ham and drippings to make sandwiches, Good Collard Greens (174), or a ham bone vegetable soup. You're dang welcome.

1 (7 to 9-pound) smoked ham, bone-in and skin on

½ cup packed light brown sugar, more as needed

1 (20-ounce) can crushed pineapple in juice, undrained

Water, as needed

½ tsp instant coffee

1. Preheat the oven to 300°F. Rinse the ham under cold water, but do not dry it off. Put the ham in a large roasting pan.

2. Rub the ham liberally with the brown sugar. Sprinkle a few more tablespoons of brown sugar in the bottom of your pan. Add the crushed pineapple and juices, pouring some over your ham and some into the pan (don't overthink it).

3. Add enough water to cover the bottom of your pan. Sprinkle in the instant coffee and stir with a fork to dissolve it in the liquid. Cover tightly with heavy-duty aluminum foil. Bake, allowing 20 minutes per pound. Baste your ham once during the last hour of cooking. Let rest for 15 minutes before slicing. Carve and serve hot with Getchyo' Man Macaroni Cheese (188), Squash Casserole (191), or Sambo's Favorite Potato Casserole (167). Add some green beans and my Sour Cream Mini Muffins (76), and you've got yourself a heavenly meal.

POTATO CHIP PORK CHOPS

MAKES 4 SERVINGS

We never ate Shake 'n Bake as kids, but this would be my version. Make sure you buy well-marbled chops from your butcher. These slap.

2 cups buttermilk

¼ cup hot sauce, such as Texas Pete or Louisiana Hot Sauce

4 well-marbled, bone-in pork chops, cut about 1-inch thick

1 (12.5-ounce) bag sour cream and onion or sweet barbecue potato chips

1 tsp salt

1 tsp freshly ground black pepper

1 tsp garlic powder

¼ tsp cayenne pepper, as desired

Olive oil in a spray bottle

1. Mix the buttermilk and hot sauce in a large bowl. Add the pork chops, seal tightly, and refrigerate for 4 to 6 hours.

2. Preheat the oven to 400°F (or see Chef's Note if using an air fryer). Pulse the potato chips in a food processor until they're a panko-like consistency. Remove the pork chops from the marinade. Season the chops on both sides with salt, pepper, garlic powder, and cayenne, as desired. Liberally coat the pork chops on all sides in the crushed chips, and rest them on a rack while your oven preheats. Spray a baking pan with oil. Place the pork chops, spaced apart, on the baking sheet and spray chops with oil as well.

3. Bake for 17 to 20 minutes, flipping halfway through. Serve hot.

CHEF'S NOTE

For Air-Fryer Pork Chops (this is my preferred method), spray the fryer basket with the oil, and preheat the air fryer to 400°F for 10 minutes. Quickly put the chops in the basket (being sure they do not touch), spritz with oil, and cook for 15 minutes.

LOW COUNTRY BOIL

MAKES 4 TO 6 SERVINGS

I hail from the Low Country, the region along the coastal plains of Georgia and South Carolina. Spanish moss hangs from live oaks so old they could tell you stories from before the Revolution. And the food is rich in flavor—deeply influenced by the Gullah Geechee African descendants who still live there. This is the OG version of what you may call a Shrimp or Crawfish Boil. You won't find any crawfish in this though. Use fresh unpeeled shrimp—Carolina or Gulf shrimp are best. Figure on at least a half pound of shrimp per person.

2 pounds uncooked jumbo shrimp (21–25 count), deveined, heads removed, unpeeled

Old Bay seasoning (or seasoned salt)

⅓ cup crab boil spice mix

1 lemon, sliced in half

2 to 3 pounds kielbasa or andouille sausage, cut into 3-inch pieces

2 to 3 pounds small red-skinned potatoes, unpeeled (the smaller the better)

6 ears fresh Silver Queen or Silver King corn (go local!), husked and halved

2 to 3 pounds snow crab (optional)

Drawn butter, cocktail sauce, and Tartar Sauce (207), in individual ramekins, for dipping

Lemon wedges, for serving

1. **Brine the shrimp:** Put the shrimp in an extra-large bowl and sprinkle liberally with Old Bay seasoning or seasoned salt. Top with enough ice to cover the shrimp. Seal the bowl tightly with aluminum foil and refrigerate for 4 to 12 hours.

2. Fill a tall 3-gallon stock pot with cold water until it comes halfway up the sides. Add the crab boil spice mix and lemon, and bring to a boil over high heat.

3. Add the sausage, cover, and cook for 10 minutes. Add the potatoes, cover, and cook until fork-tender (about 10 minutes). Add the corn, cover, and cook about 6 minutes. Add the snow crab, if using. Cover and cook until heated through, about 5 minutes. Drain the shrimp, add to the pot, cover, and turn off the heat. Cook just until they turn pink, 3 to 5 minutes, depending on the size of the shrimp. Do not overcook the shrimp.

4. Using long tongs and a wire sieve, transfer the ingredients to a large platter. Serve hot, with drawn butter, cocktail sauce, tartar sauce, and lemon wedges. Try the boil with Garlic Cheddar Butter Biscuits (75) or Beer Cheese Bread (80).

BISCUIT BLTS WITH PIMENTO CHEESE

MAKES 1 SANDWICH

If I were on death row, I'd request this for breakfast, though you can serve it anytime. For the love, use my Cathead Biscuits (72) and Pimento Cheese (41) recipes. The marriage of textures and flavors is on point. Start frying your bacon when you put the biscuits in the oven, and have everything ready to go so the biscuits don't get cold. And I don't bother with the lettuce.

2 slices thick-cut bacon, preferably peppered

1 large egg

1 Cathead Biscuit, (72), sliced in half

2 T Pimento Cheese (41), heated in the microwave for a few seconds just until spreadable

Homegrown tomato, sliced

Salt, to taste

Freshly ground black pepper, to taste

1. Heat a medium skillet, preferably cast iron, over medium heat until hot. Add the bacon and cook, turning once, until crisp and browned, about 7 to 8 minutes. Transfer to paper towels to drain, leaving the fat in the skillet.

2. Fry an egg over-medium in the bacon drippings. (For over-medium, cook until the whites are set, 1 to 1 ½ minutes. Flip the egg and cook it for another 5 to 30 seconds, to your liking.) Get the biscuit ready as the egg fries. Spread the biscuit bottom with the pimento cheese. Microwave on high for about 10 seconds (or use a toaster oven) until the cheese is melting.

3. Add sliced, homegrown tomato (salt and pepper it, we're not animals), and then add the bacon, broken into half-sized pieces. Add the egg, and cap with the biscuit top. Serve immediately with plenty of napkins.

ROCKSTAR CABBAGE

MAKES 4 TO 6 SERVINGS

I lived off this in college. (Go Dawgs.) It's a quick one-dish meal, 'cause you've got rockstar things to do. Tastes great with pork or turkey keilbasa. Serve it with Buttermilk Cornbread (71), Savannah Red Rice (190), or roasted potatoes if you're feelin' skinny. Tastes even better the next day.

1 T olive oil or bacon grease, plus more as needed

1 pound pork or turkey kielbasa, cut into bite-size chunks

1 large sweet onion, sliced

2 garlic cloves, minced

1 head green cabbage, about 2 ½ pounds, cored and cut into 1-inch shreds

⅓ cup Rich Chicken Stock (64) or store-bought or water

Salt, to taste

Freshly ground black pepper, to taste

1 T cider vinegar

1 T light brown sugar

1. Heat the oil in a large skillet over medium-high heat. Add the kielbasa and cook, stirring occasionally, until browned. Transfer to a bowl. Reserve drippings in the pan.

2. Reduce heat to medium. Add the onions and a touch more oil. Cook the onions for 2 to 3 minutes or until they begin to tenderize. Add the garlic, cabbage, stock, salt, and lots of black pepper. Cover, stirring occasionally, until the cabbage has wilted, about 5 to 7 minutes. Stir in the vinegar and brown sugar.

3. Cover tightly and cook until the cabbage is tender, about 10 to 15 minutes, stirring occasionally. The cabbage will become softer the longer it's cooked, so adjust the cook time to your preferences. After 10 to 15 minutes, remove the lid, stir, and allow some of the liquid to evaporate. (Add a few pats of salted butter if you're not counting calories.) Stir in the cooked kielbasa. Serve hot.

This dish can be stored in the fridge in a covered container for up to 6 days.

OVEN-FRIED CANE BUTTER CHICKEN

MAKES 4 TO 6 SERVINGS

Summer of my fifth-grade year, Mama required us to plan and prepare one meal each week, under her supervision. By the time we graduated high school, we were some domestic little hoochies. Here's my version of the first dish my sister ever made. This is date night *gold*. But if they flinch at bone-in chicken? Red flag.

SEASONED CHICKEN

¼ cup (½ stick) butter

1 tsp salt

1 tsp garlic powder

½ tsp freshly ground black pepper

¼ tsp celery salt

⅛ tsp cayenne pepper

6 chicken thighs, bone-in and skin on

SEASONED FLOUR

1 cup all-purpose flour

1 tsp garlic powder

1 tsp celery salt

1 tsp sweet paprika

½ tsp sugar

¼ tsp ground white pepper

⅛ tsp cayenne pepper

CANE BUTTER SAUCE

¼ cup (½ stick) salted butter, melted

¼ cup cane syrup or honey

1 T fresh lemon juice

1. Preheat the oven to 400°F. Place the butter in a 9 x 13-inch baking dish and pop it in the oven during preheating.

2. **Season the chicken:** Combine the salt, garlic powder, black pepper, celery salt, and cayenne in a small bowl, and season the chicken on both sides. Set aside.

3. **Season the flour:** In a medium bowl, whisk the flour, garlic powder, celery salt, paprika, sugar, white pepper, and cayenne to combine. Coat the chicken well in the flour mixture, and add to the dish of melted butter. Flip to coat with butter, leaving thighs skin-side down. Bake for 20 to 30 minutes.

4. **Make the cane butter sauce:** Whisk the melted butter, cane syrup, and lemon juice. Once chicken has baked, remove from oven, turn your chicken skin-side up, and pour the cane butter sauce over the chicken. Bake another 20 to 30 minutes. Let rest 5 to 10 minutes before serving.

GETCHYO' MAN FRIED CHICKEN FINGERS

MAKES 2 TO 3 SERVINGS

I love fried chicken almost as much as I love Jesus. Here's an easy version that won't stink up your kitchen or bloat your tummy. Plus, the air fryer makes this so easy! (If you don't have an air fryer, I've got you covered, Shoog. See the Chef's Note). Serve with Honey Mustard (205), duh.

2 cups buttermilk

3 T hot sauce, such as Texas Pete or Louisiana Hot Sauce

2 tsp salt, divided

1 tsp sugar, divided

1 pound chicken breast tenderloins

½ cup self-rising flour, preferably White Lily

½ cup all-purpose flour

1 tsp garlic powder

1 tsp black pepper

½ tsp celery salt

½ tsp cayenne pepper

Neutral oil, in a spray bottle

1. Whisk the buttermilk, hot sauce, 1 teaspoon salt, and ½ teaspoon of sugar in a medium bowl. Add the tenderloins and toss to cover. Seal with plastic wrap and refrigerate for at least 30 minutes and up to 2 hours (the longer the better).

2. Place a wire cooling rack over a baking sheet. Whisk the self-rising flour, all-purpose flour, remaining 1 teaspoon salt, remaining ½ teaspoon sugar, garlic powder, black pepper, celery salt, and cayenne in a deep-dish pie pan. Toss each tenderloin in the flour to coat and place on the wire rack. Let rest for 10 minutes to set. Spritz the tops with olive oil.

3. Preheat your air fryer to 400°F. Spritz your air fryer tray with oil. Quickly arrange a few tenders on the tray so they're not touching, and fry for 12 minutes. Serve hot with Honey Mustard (205) for dipping and literally anything from my Sides chapter.

CHEF'S NOTE

If using an oven, preheat to 450°F. Mist a large-rimmed baking sheet with oil. Arrange the tenderloins well-apart on the baking sheet, and generously spray the tops with oil. Bake for 6 minutes. Flip the tenderloins and cook until golden brown and cooked through, 6 to 8 minutes more.

Or, if you're going low-carb, try coating the tenders with a mixture of crushed pork rinds or almond meal and grated Parmesan. Use gluten-free flour if that rocks your boat.

WHITE CHICKEN CHILI

MAKES 6 TO 8 SERVINGS

This is an easy one-pot meal—perfect for serving a bunch of folks in a hurry. Here's my version.

3 T olive oil

2 pounds boneless, skinless chicken breast or thighs, cut into bite-size pieces

1 medium white onion, chopped

2 garlic cloves, finely chopped

1 tsp salt

1 tsp Aleppo pepper or chili powder

½ tsp garlic powder

½ tsp onion powder

¼ tsp ground white pepper

½ tsp black pepper

¼ tsp cumin

¼ tsp cayenne pepper

1 quart (about 4 cups) Rich Chicken Stock (64) or store-bought stock

1 (7-ounce) can diced green chiles, undrained

3 (15-ounce) cans Great Northern beans, drained and rinsed

1 cup sour cream, plus more for serving

Fresh cilantro, for garnish

1. Heat the oil in a large Dutch oven over medium heat. Add the chicken, onion, and garlic and cook, stirring occasionally, until the chicken no longer looks raw and the onion is softened, about 6 minutes. Sprinkle in salt, Aleppo pepper, garlic powder, onion powder, white pepper, black pepper, cumin, and cayenne, and stir well. Add the stock and bring to a boil, scraping up all that good stuff on the bottom of the pot. Stir in the chiles and beans and return to a boil.

2. Reduce the heat to low. Cover and simmer, stirring occasionally, for 20 to 30 minutes. When ready to serve, stir in the sour cream. Garnish with the cilantro and more sour cream if desired. Serve with Buttermilk Cornbread (71) or Sour Cream Mini Muffins (76).

IN A DASH: You can also substitute 4 cups cooked and chopped meat from a rotisserie chicken for the freshly cooked chicken.

VEGGIE CHILI

MAKES 8 TO 10 SERVINGS

I love cooking soul food for my vegan friends. Serve with a hearty jalapeño cornbread.

2 T olive oil

3 bell peppers (preferably red, orange, and yellow), seeded and chopped

1 large white or yellow onion, chopped

2 jalapeño peppers, seeded and finely chopped (include some seeds and ribs if you like it spicy)

Salt, to taste

Freshly ground black pepper, to taste

1 garlic clove, minced

1 (28-ounce) can petite diced tomatoes, undrained

1 (28-ounce) can crushed tomatoes

⅓ cup beer, such as lager (not IPA)

1 sweet potato, peeled and chopped in 1-inch cubes

1 (6-ounce) can tomato paste

2 (16-ounce) cans chili beans in spicy chili sauce

2 (15-ounce) cans black beans, drained

3 T chili powder

3 T light brown sugar

2 T yellow mustard

½ tsp ground cumin

½ tsp garlic powder

¼ tsp cayenne pepper

¼ cup instant potato flakes

Vegan sour cream, for garnish

Fresh cilantro, for garnish

1. In a large Dutch oven, heat the oil over medium-high heat. Add the bell peppers, onion, and jalapeños and cook until tender, about 4 minutes. Season with salt and pepper to taste, to sweat the vegetables. Add the garlic and cook until fragrant, about 1 minute.

2. Add the diced tomatoes with their juices and the crushed tomatoes. Rinse out the tomato cans with the beer and add to the pot. Add the sweet potatoes. Add the tomato paste and stir to dissolve.

3. Stir in the chili beans and black beans, chili powder, brown sugar, mustard, cumin, garlic powder, and cayenne. Salt to taste, and mix well. Bring to a boil over medium-high heat. Reduce the heat to low and cover. Simmer for 30 to 40 minutes, stirring occasionally to ensure that the beans don't stick to the bottom.

4. Lastly, stir in potato flakes to thicken. Enjoy with a dollop of vegan sour cream and fresh cilantro. Serve with cornbread (vegan, of course).

MAN CHILI

MAKES 6 SERVINGS

When you hear *chili*, yeah . . . you probably picture Kevin from *The Office* fumbling that big ol' pot (bless it). I dropped this bad boy on TikTok one night, and the next thing I know— Kevin himself, Brian Baumgartner, put it in his *Seriously Good Chili Cookbook*. Folks been tellin' me they're winning cook-offs with this recipe . . . I'm flattered. Now, y'all pay up that prize money!

1 pound ground chuck

1 pound pork sausage, mild or spicy

1 medium yellow onion, chopped

2 jalapeño peppers, seeded and finely chopped (include some seeds and ribs if you like it spicy)

1 (28-ounce) can petite diced tomatoes, undrained

1 (28-ounce) can crushed tomatoes

⅓ cup beer, such as lager (not IPA)

1 (6-ounce) can tomato paste

2 (16-ounce) cans chili beans in spicy chili sauce

1 (15-ounce) can black beans, drained

2 ½ T chili powder

2 T light brown sugar

2 T prepared yellow mustard

1 tsp salt

½ tsp ground cumin

½ tsp garlic powder

¼ tsp cayenne pepper

¼ cup instant potato flakes

Sour cream or Pimento Cheese (41), for serving

1. Heat a large Dutch oven over medium-high heat. Add the ground chuck and sausage, and brown the meat, breaking it up with a wooden spoon, about 10 minutes. Drain the meat in a colander set over a bowl to reserve the drippings. Reduce heat to medium-low, return about 3 tablespoons of drippings to the pot, add the onion and jalapeños, and cook for 3 to 4 minutes.

2. Add the diced tomatoes and the crushed tomatoes. Rinse out the tomato cans with the beer and add to the pot. Add the tomato paste and stir to dissolve. Return the drained meat to the pot, and add the chili beans, black beans, chili powder, brown sugar, mustard, salt, cumin, garlic powder, and cayenne. Bring to a simmer. Reduce the heat to low, and cover. Simmer for 30 minutes, stirring occasionally so the chili doesn't stick.

3. Stir in the potato flakes to thicken the chili, and simmer for a few minutes longer. Season with salt. Serve hot with a dollop of sour cream or Pimento Cheese (41).

CHEF'S NOTE

FOR A LEANER VERSION, MAKE TURKEY CHILI: Heat 2 tablespoons olive oil in the Dutch oven over medium-high heat. Add 2 pounds ground turkey (93% lean) and cook, stirring occasionally and breaking up the meat with a wooden spoon until browned, about 7 minutes. Transfer the cooked turkey to a bowl while you cook your onion and peppers in the same pot. Add 2 tablespoons olive oil to the pot to cook the onion and jalapeños. Continue to Step 2.

TULSA CHICKEN 'N' GRAVY

MAKES 4 SERVINGS

They take good care of us when we play in Tulsa. My band and I always request this dish at catering. Here's my easy version of this chicken and milk gravy. You can use breasts or thighs.

6 T salted butter

1 pound chicken tenderloins, pounded to ¾-inch thick

1 ½ tsp salt, divided

¾ tsp freshly ground black pepper, divided

1 ½ tsp garlic powder, divided

1 cup all-purpose flour

1 tsp smoked paprika

½ tsp sugar

1 cup whole milk, as needed

1. Preheat the oven to 350°F. Melt the butter in a 9 x 13-inch baking dish for a few minutes while the oven preheats. Don't let it burn.

2. Cover the chicken with plastic wrap, and pound to approximately ¾-inch thick. Season cutlets liberally with ½ teaspoon salt, ¼ teaspoon black pepper, and ½ teaspoon garlic powder. (You know how we do.)

3. In a deep pie dish, mix the remaining 1 teaspoon salt, remaining ½ teaspoon black pepper, remaining 1 teaspoon garlic powder, flour, paprika, and sugar. Press the tenderloins in the flour mixture to coat well, then lay them flat in the dish of melted butter, spacing them out a tad. Add enough milk until the chicken is almost covered (you won't use a whole cup). Sprinkle the milky areas with 2 to 3 tablespoons of the remaining seasoned flour.

4. Bake until the sauce is thickened and the chicken has lightly browned, about 25 to 30 minutes. Serve with Easy Roasted Veggies (185) and garlic mashed potatoes.

"MA, THE MEATLOAF!"

MAKES 8 SERVINGS

I say this title in my best Will Ferrell voice. Haters can come at me, but I actually prefer this dish with ground turkey. This is great to cook at the top of the week for meal prep! Serve this with mashed potatoes or cauliflower mash and Getchyo' Man Garden Peas (181), please.

1 T olive oil, plus more for the loaf pan

1 large yellow onion, chopped

½ green bell pepper, seeded and chopped

2 garlic cloves, minced

½ cup Rich Beef Stock (65) or reduced-sodium store-bought stock

½ cup plain breadcrumbs

¼ cup whole milk or evaporated milk

2 pounds ground turkey or ground beef

2 large eggs, beaten

2 T Worcestershire sauce

2 tsp salt

½ tsp freshly ground black pepper

3 T ketchup, divided

2 T yellow mustard, divided

1. Heat the oil in a large skillet over medium heat. Add the onion, bell pepper, and garlic and cook for 1 minute. Stir in the stock and cook until the vegetables are tender and most of the stock has evaporated, about 4 minutes. Remove from the heat and let cool.

2. Preheat the oven to 375°F. Line a 9 x 5-inch loaf pan with aluminum foil. In a large bowl, soak the breadcrumbs in the milk for a few minutes. Add the turkey (or beef), cooled vegetables, eggs, Worcestershire sauce, salt, and pepper. Add 1 tablespoon each of ketchup and mustard. Mix with your hands until combined. Pat the meat into the prepared pan. Mix the remaining 2 tablespoons ketchup and 1 tablespoon mustard and spread over the top.

3. Bake until the top is browned, about 1 hour. Let the loaf stand for a few minutes. Slice and serve hot.

CHICKEN PIE

MAKES 2 PIES, 6 TO 8 SERVINGS EACH

This Dasher family recipe is more than seven generations old. I grew up eating chicken pie at every covered dish dinner at Laurel Hill Lutheran Church (Lorrrd, can those Salzburgers cook!). Here's my version of Grandma's recipe—minus her homemade piecrust. Who's got time for that? This recipe freezes well.

¼ cup (½ stick) salted butter

1 large sweet onion, such as Vidalia, chopped

2 to 3 celery ribs, chopped (1 cup)

Salt, to taste

Freshly ground black pepper, to taste

¾ cup all-purpose flour

2 cups Rich Chicken Stock (64) or quality store-bought stock

4 hard-boiled eggs, peeled and chopped into bite-size pieces

8 cups chopped rotisserie chicken

2 (14.1-ounce) packages refrigerated rolled piecrusts (4 crusts)

1. Preheat the oven to 350°F. Melt the butter in a large saucepan over medium heat. Add the onion and celery and cook until softened, about 4 minutes. Season with salt and pepper. We're not animals. Sprinkle in the flour, and stir to coat everything in the pan. Gradually whisk in 2 cups of stock and bring to a simmer. Reduce the heat to low and simmer until thickened, about 5 minutes. Turn off the heat. Stir the chopped boiled eggs and chicken into the gravy mixture.

2. Line two deep-dish pie pans with one piecrust each. Divide the filling between the pans. Top each with an additional piecrust. Seal the sides with a fork. Cut a slit in the top of each piecrust to vent the steam. Tent the tops of the pies with aluminum foil, and bake until the crusts are golden brown, about 60 to 70 minutes. Serve hot.

⁂ CHEF'S NOTE

If cooking your chicken from scratch, refer to the method on Rich Chicken Stock (64). Reduce your cook time to 30 to 40 minutes, or until your chicken reaches an internal temperature of 165°F.

Make the whole recipe so you have one pie to freeze for an easy future meal or one to give away to someone who might not be cooking for themselves. Here's how: after Step 2, allow the mixture to cool. Place the filling in deep-dish aluminum pie pans so they're freezer- and oven-safe. Wrap the pies tightly with plastic wrap and then wrap in heavy foil, and place in a jumbo airtight freezer bag. Freeze for up to 3 months.

CHICKEN SCALLOP

MAKES 2 CASSEROLES, 6 TO 8 SERVINGS EACH

This makes chicken spaghetti feel shame. This was Grandma's recipe. It fits perfectly in two deep-dish pie pans—one for you, one for a friend or the freezer.

8 ounces egg noodles

¼ cup (½ stick) butter

1 large yellow onion, chopped

½ large green bell pepper, seeded and chopped

2 celery ribs, chopped (1 cup)

Salt, to taste

Freshly ground black pepper, to taste

¼ cup all-purpose flour

2 ½ cups whole milk

⅛ tsp cayenne pepper, optional

1 rotisserie chicken, deboned, deskinned, and chopped, or 4 cups white and dark meat, cooked, seasoned, and chopped

1 ½ cups small curd cottage cheese

1 (4-ounce) jar diced pimentos, drained

2 cups freshly shredded sharp cheddar, divided

Sweet or smoked paprika, for garnish

1. Preheat the oven to 350°F. Cook the egg noodles according to the package directions in salted water. Drain and rinse in a colander and set aside.

2. Melt the butter in an extra-large skillet over medium heat. Add the onion, green pepper, and celery and cook, until softened, about 4 minutes. Salt and pepper the veggies. Reduce heat to medium-low, and sprinkle in the flour, stirring well to coat the veggies. Gradually whisk in the milk until the mixture is smooth and thickened, about 5 minutes. Add salt and pepper to taste and cayenne pepper, if using. Remove from the heat and stir in the chicken, cottage cheese, and pimentos, followed by the cooked egg noodles. Divide the filling between the prepared pans. Top each with 1 cup of cheddar and a sprinkle of paprika.

3. Bake until bubbling, about 45 to 50 minutes. Serve hot.

CHEF'S NOTE

Make the whole recipe so you have one to freeze for an easy future meal or one to give away to someone who might not be cooking for themselves. After Step 2, allow the mixture to cool. Spread in a deep-dish aluminum pie pan that is freezer- and oven-safe. Wrap tightly with plastic wrap and then wrap in heavy aluminum foil, and place in a jumbo airtight freezer bag. Freeze for up to 3 months.

FRIED CHICKEN LIVERS WITH PORT WINE SAUCE

MAKES 6 SERVINGS

Do *not* turn your nose up—*especially if you don't eat chicken livers*. I had somethin' like this one Christmas Eve at Vic's on the River in Savannah and about passed out. Went home and re-created it from memory. And baby . . . this'll eat. Serve it over grits, lumpy mashed potatoes, or cauliflower mash. This sauce? Try it with duck breast or beef tenderloin too. Some bing cherries . . . trust me.

FRIED LIVERS

20 ounces chicken livers

1 tsp salt, plus more for sprinkling

1 cup buttermilk

1 large egg

1 ¼ cups self-rising flour, White Lily preferred

1 tsp freshly ground black pepper

1 tsp garlic powder

½ tsp granulated sugar

¼ tsp cayenne pepper

Peanut oil, for frying

PORT WINE SAUCE

⅓ cup shallot or red onion, minced

Salt, to taste

Freshly ground black pepper, to taste

1 cup port wine

1 cup Rich Beef Stock (65) or store-bought stock

2 T balsamic reduction

1 to 2 tsp light brown sugar, as needed, optional

2 to 3 T cold unsalted butter, thinly sliced

1. **Make the livers:** Rinse and drain the livers. Place them in a bowl, poke each liver a few times with a fork, and sprinkle with salt.

2. Grab a wire rack, a medium bowl, and a pie dish. In the bowl, whisk together the buttermilk and egg. Add the livers and let them soak. In the pie dish, mix the self-rising flour, 1 teaspoon salt, pepper, garlic powder, granulated sugar, and cayenne. A few at a time, dredge the livers in the seasoned flour to coat, then place them on the rack to rest for 10 minutes.

3. Line a covered baking dish with paper towels (I use my Corningware). Pour oil into a large cast iron skillet to a depth

of about 1 inch. Heat over medium to medium-high heat until the oil reaches 325°F on a deep-frying thermometer. Working in batches to avoid crowding the pan, fry the livers for 2 to 3 minutes per side. The livers will pop as they cook, so use a lid to protect yourself. Transfer the livers to the paper towel–lined dish, sprinkle with salt, and cover with the lid to keep them warm as you fry the remaining batches.

4. **Make the port wine sauce:** Reduce heat to medium-low and discard all but 2 tablespoons of the drippings. To the same skillet, add the shallot (or onion) and cook, stirring often, until softened, about 2 minutes. Season with salt and pepper to taste. Whisk in the port wine, beef stock, balsamic reduction, and brown sugar. Bring to a simmer, and cook until the volume has reduced by half, about 5 minutes. Taste and add more brown sugar if the sauce is too tart. Remove from the heat and whisk in the butter until the sauce is smooth and glossy.

5. Add the livers to the sauce, making sure they're as submerged as possible. Return the skillet to the burner over medium-low, and simmer gently for 5 to 7 minutes. Serve immediately over smashed cauliflower or Proper Grits (187).

FRIED CATFISH PO'BOYS

MAKES 3 SANDWICHES

Back up, Owen Han . . . this is my favorite sandwich evuhhh. This is catfish with soul that just happens to be sittin' on bread. Make sure you're buying actual catfish, though, and not one of its trashy cousins.

Neutral oil, in a spray bottle

2 large eggs

2 tsp hot sauce, such as Texas Pete or Louisiana Hot Sauce

⅔ cup yellow cornmeal

¼ cup all-purpose flour

3 T Provider Sonora seasoning (see Chef's Note)

1 T sugar

½ tsp salt

¼ tsp freshly ground black pepper

3 catfish fillets, skinned

Vegetable oil, for frying

3 fresh hoagie rolls, split

6 T Tartar Sauce (207)

1 cup shredded iceberg lettuce

6 tomato slices

1. Lightly mist a baking sheet with oil. In a deep-dish pie plate, whisk the eggs and hot sauce. In a brown paper bag, put the cornmeal, flour, Sonora seasoning, sugar, salt, and black pepper and shake the shit out of it to combine. One at a time, dip the catfish fillets in the egg mixture. Then drop 'em into the brown bag and shake to coat. Place the filets on the prepared baking sheet and refrigerate for 15 minutes. (Trust me here. This sets the crust.)

2. Line a plate with paper towels. Pour oil into a heavy skillet to a depth of 1 inch. Add the catfish and fry until golden brown, about 2 to 3 minutes on each side. Using tongs, transfer the fish to the paper towels, to drain briefly.

3. For each po'boy, slather a hoagie with 2 tablespoons (or more) of tartar sauce. Add a catfish fillet, a handful of lettuce, and two tomato slices. Serve with Daddy's Coleslaw (169), or omit the bread and serve the fish with slaw and Proper Grits (187). Yum.

CHEF'S NOTE

You can make a substitute for the Provider's Sonora seasoning: 1 teaspoon garlic powder, 1 teaspoon onion powder, 1 teaspoon Aleppo pepper powder, 1 teaspoon salt, 1 teaspoon sugar, 1 teaspoon smoked paprika, 1 teaspoon chili powder, ½ teaspoon cayenne, and a scant ½ teaspoon cumin.

MAMA'S TOMATO PIE

MAKES 8 SERVINGS

Simple and fancy at the same time. If you can't get homegrown tomatoes, buy Campari tomatoes. You don't have to peel them. Serve this for lunch, brunch, or as a side dish. This one's inspired by my hot mama.

5 ripe Campari tomatoes, thinly sliced (about ½-inch)

Salt, for sprinkling

1 frozen deep-dish piecrust, thawed, pierced with a fork

1 heaping cup mayonnaise

⅓ cup grated Parmesan

1 large egg

2 cups shredded sharp Vermont white cheddar, divided

¼ cup plain breadcrumbs

2 tsp brown sugar

4 slices thick-cut bacon, cooked until crisp, cooled and crumbled

1 medium sweet onion, such as Vidalia, chopped

1. Preheat the oven to 425°F. Lightly sprinkle the tomatoes with salt on both sides. Place on baking sheets lined with paper towels, and cover with more paper towels. Let the tomatoes sweat on the baking sheet for about 30 minutes.

2. Line a deep-dish pie plate with the piecrust. Poke holes in the crust with a fork, top with foil, and fill with dried beans or uncooked rice. Bake 7 to 8 minutes. Remove the foil and the beans or rice, and set the crust aside. Reduce the oven temperature to 350°F.

3. In a medium bowl, whisk to combine the mayonnaise, Parmesan, and egg. Mix in 1 cup of the shredded cheddar.

4. Sprinkle the breadcrumbs in the bottom of the piecrust. Top with half of the tomatoes and sprinkle with half of the brown sugar, bacon, and onion. Spread with half of the mayonnaise mixture. Repeat layers and top with the remaining cheese. Tent the crust with foil. Bake about 35 to 40 minutes. Serve warm.

Sides

SAMBO'S FAVORITE POTATO CASSEROLE
DADDY'S COLESLAW
SAUSAGE DRESSING
BUTTER BEANS 'N' DUMPLIN'S
CAULIFLOWER AU GRATIN
GOOD COLLARD GREENS
BRUNSWICK STEW
BUSY GIRL GREEN BEANS
GETCHYO' MAN GARDEN PEAS
SQUASH FRITTERS
EASY ROASTED VEGGIES
PROPER GRITS
GETCHYO' MAN MACARONI CHEESE
SAVANNAH RED RICE
SQUASH CASSEROLE
YOU AIN'T NEVUH HAD THESE BLACK-EYED PEAS

SAMBO'S FAVORITE POTATO CASSEROLE

MAKES 8 TO 10 SERVINGS

It's hard to mess up a hash-brown casserole, but most folks use canned soup, and you know how I feel about that. Try it this way, and you'll never go back again. Hank Jr.'s son, Sam, once ate half of a casserole in one sitting at my house. This one's for you, Sambo. Love yew!

CASSEROLE

1 medium yellow onion, finely chopped

2 cups From-Scratch Cream of Chicken Soup (67) or Cream of Mushroom Soup (69)

1 cup sour cream

½ cup (1 stick) salted butter, melted

2 cups (16 ounces) freshly shredded sharp cheddar

¼ teaspoon garlic powder

Salt, to taste

Freshly ground black pepper, to taste

1 (32-ounce) bag frozen hash browns (cubed)

TOPPING

1 heaping cup Corn Flakes, uncrushed, or sour cream and cheddar potato chips, crushed

¼ cup (½ stick) salted butter, melted

1. **Make the casserole:** Preheat the oven to 350°F. In a large mixing bowl, mix the onion, soup, sour cream, melted butter, cheddar, and garlic powder. Season with salt and pepper, to taste. Fold in the hash browns until everything's acquainted, and spread into a 9 x 13-inch baking dish.

2. **Make the topping:** In a small bowl, toss the Corn Flakes (or crushed potato chips) and melted butter and scatter over the casserole.

3. Bake until browned, about 1 hour. Serve hot.

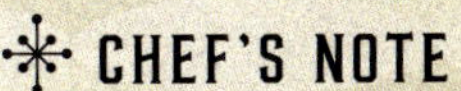

CHEF'S NOTE

Pairs well with my Man Chili (143) or Veggie Chili (142). Scoop a healthy dollop of this casserole on top like it's ice cream on a cobbler. You're welcome.

DADDY'S COLESLAW

MAKES 6 TO 8 SERVINGS

Pull up, KFC! This slaw is my favorite. Pair it with Fried Catfish Po'boys (158) or Low Country Boil (130).

- ½ cup mayonnaise
- ¼ cup sugar
- 1 T yellow onion, minced
- 1 T white vinegar
- 1 tsp salt
- ½ tsp freshly ground black pepper
- ¼ tsp celery seed
- 1 (14 to 16-ounce) bag coleslaw mix or ½ medium head green cabbage, cored and shredded
- ¼ cup shredded carrots (optional)

Whisk the mayonnaise, sugar, onion, vinegar, salt, pepper, and celery seed in a large bowl to dissolve the sugar. Add the coleslaw mix and carrots, if using. Mix well and let stand for 20 minutes before serving.

The coleslaw can be covered and refrigerated for up to 3 days.

SAUSAGE DRESSING

MAKES 8 TO 10 SERVINGS

Stuffing's for your bra . . . *dressing's* for your dinner plate. Here's a great way to use up leftover sausage gravy, biscuits, and my From-Scratch Cream of Chicken Soup (67) or From-Scratch Cream of Mushroom Soup (69). Cornbread and biscuits can be made a day or two ahead.

2 pounds sage pork sausage

2 cups celery, chopped

2 cups onion, chopped (preferably yellow or Vidalia sweet)

¼ cup (½ stick) salted butter

Salt, to taste

Freshly ground black pepper, to taste

2 to 3 T flour

2 ½ cups half-and-half

¼ tsp white pepper

¼ tsp dried sage

½ tsp garlic powder

4 to 5 Cathead Biscuits (72)

1 pan Buttermilk Cornbread (71) (unsweetened)

2 cups Rich Ham Stock (66)

2 cups Rich Chicken Stock (64), or more as needed

1. Preheat the oven to 350°F. Heat a large skillet over medium heat. Add the sausage and break it into chunks (about 2 inches in diameter). Stir only occasionally, allowing the meat to crust and brown on each side, about 7 to 8 minutes. Do not burn. Transfer to a paper towel–lined colander to drain.

2. Make the Cream of Soup Mixture: In the same pan, add the celery, onion, and butter. Salt and pepper to taste. Cook over medium-low heat for 4 minutes or until tender.

3. Sprinkle on flour and stir to coat contents of the pan. Once flour begins to take on some color, about 2 minutes, add the half-and-half. Reduce heat to low and whisk until smooth. Season with white pepper, sage, garlic powder, more salt and black pepper, if desired, and allow to simmer for a few minutes to thicken. Turn off heat.

4. In a large mixing bowl, break up your biscuits and cornbread into large chunks. Add your sausage, cream of soup mixture, and ham stock, and stir to combine. Add enough chicken stock so the contents of the bowl jiggle when shaken. If a spoon can stand straight up on its own, you need a little more stock. Pour the mixture into a large casserole dish and bake until golden brown, about 35 to 40 minutes. Serve warm.

The baked dressing can be refrigerated for up to 4 days. To freeze, pour the unbaked dressing into aluminum casserole pans and wrap tightly with plastic wrap and heavy-duty foil. Place in a jumbo freezer bag and freeze for up to 12 months. Thaw in the fridge for 24 to 48 hours prior to baking.

BUTTER BEANS 'N' DUMPLIN'S

MAKES 6 TO 8 SERVINGS

My nana hasn't been to church since the 1970s 'cause someone pissed her off in Sunday school. But Mama said you could always find these on the table at home and at Middle Ground Baptist Church dinners when she was growing up. It was at this church where I gave my heart to Jesus. One bite of Nana's Butter Beans 'n' Dumplin's, and you'll wanna rededicate your life too.

BUTTER BEANS

7 ounces salt pork (streak o' lean) or salted fatback

1 (24-ounce) bag frozen butter beans

½ tsp freshly ground black pepper

DUMPLIN'S

2 cups self-rising flour, plus more for rolling

1 large egg

¼ tsp salt

¾ cup whole milk, as needed

1. **Make the butter beans:** Bring a medium saucepan or pot of water to a boil. Meanwhile, cut the salt pork into 2-inch chunks, and rinse it well to remove some of the salt. Add the pork to the water and boil for 3 minutes. Drain.

2. To the same pot with the pork, add the butter beans and pepper, along with enough fresh cold water to cover contents by 2 inches or so. Bring to a boil over high heat. Reduce the heat to medium-low and cover. Simmer until the beans and pork are tender, about 20 minutes.

3. **Make the dumplin's:** Add flour to a small mixing bowl and make a well in the center with your fist. Add the egg, salt, and a splash of milk (you won't use all the flour—it will create a barrier around the bowl to keep the dough from sticking). Use your fingers to burst the yolk and lightly stir the contents, gradually pulling in a little flour from the sides. Add milk as needed until a thin, soft, biscuit-like dough has formed.

4. Lightly dust your clean counter with flour, and transfer the dough to the counter. Sprinkle a little flour on top of the dough, and using a floured rolling pin, roll the dough to about ¼-inch thick. Cut into 2 x 2-inch squares.

5. Taste the pot liquor (that's the broth, Linda) for salt. It should be tasty and well-seasoned. Add the dumplin's on top of the beans. Simmer uncovered until the dumplin's are risen and cooked through, 10 to 12 minutes. The dough will thicken the pot liquor. Serve hot or warm.

CAULIFLOWER AU GRATIN

MAKES 4 TO 6 SERVINGS

Papa wore Liberty overalls, could cut a rug, and cooked just enough to keep you impressed. He used to make a cauliflower au gratin when we were kids. I whipped this up from memory and now make it on the regular. This dish looks fancy, but it's *sooo* easy.

CAULIFLOWER

1 large head cauliflower, green leaves removed

Salt, to taste

Freshly ground black pepper, to taste

2 T salted butter, melted

CHEESE SAUCE

¼ cup (½ stick) salted butter

1 T grated yellow onion (use the large holes on a box grater)

2 to 3 T all-purpose flour

2 cups half-and-half or whole milk

1 cup (8 ounces) shredded sharp cheddar

¼ tsp white pepper

1. **Cook the cauliflower:** Preheat the oven to 350°F. Place the cauliflower in a large pot of heavily salted water. Bring to a boil and simmer until the cauliflower is fork-tender, about 10 to 15 minutes. Drain well and cut the cauliflower into fourths, if desired. Transfer to a deep oval Pyrex or 9 x 9-inch baking dish. Season with salt and pepper and drizzle with the melted butter.

2. **Make the cheese sauce:** Melt the butter in a medium saucepan or pot over medium-low heat. Add the grated onion and cook for 1 minute. Sprinkle in the flour and whisk until smooth. Once the flour has taken on color, about 1 minute, add the half-and-half. Cook until thickened and bubbling, about 3 minutes. Turn off the heat and whisk in ⅔ of the cheese and white pepper. Salt and pepper to taste.

3. Pour the cheese sauce over the cauliflower. Top with the remaining cheese and bake until bubbly, about 20 minutes. Serve hot.

GOOD COLLARD GREENS

MAKES 10 TO 12 SERVINGS

I'd call these Getchyo' Man Greens, but collards tend to smell like a poot. Put an unshelled pecan in the pot to absorb the odor. These are the best I've eaten. This recipe's a great use of that leftover bone from your Sund'y Ham (127), or if you have any cabbage, shred it and add to the pot. Daddy does this, and it's bomb.

1 leftover ham with bone, meat, and pan juices

2 pounds fresh collard greens, washed and trimmed, or 2 (16-ounce) bags pre-washed collard greens

¼ cup cider vinegar

¼ cup brown sugar, plus more to taste

2 T hot sauce, such as Texas Pete or Louisiana Hot Sauce, plus more to taste

1 (15-ounce) can crushed tomatoes (optional)

1 to 2 quarts (4 to 8 cups) Rich Ham Stock (66) or Rich Chicken Stock (64), as needed

Salt, to taste

Freshly ground black pepper, to taste

1. In a large, tall stock pot with a lid, add the leftover ham—bone, meat, juices, and all. Add the greens, vinegar, brown sugar, hot sauce, and crushed tomatoes (if using). Use a large spoon to press everything down tightly into the pot. Pour in enough stock to just cover the greens. Bring to a boil over high heat.

2. Reduce the heat to medium low, cover, and simmer, about 30 to 40 minutes. Remove the lid and continue simmering for approximately 1 hour or until the greens are very tender. Season with salt and pepper, to taste, and more brown sugar and hot sauce if desired.

If you don't have a leftover ham, use the Ham Hock Method below.

3 ham hocks

1 quart (4 cups) Rich Chicken Stock (64)

1 medium onion, diced

2 garlic cloves, chopped

1 T sugar

Salt, to taste

Freshly ground black pepper, to taste

1. Add ham hocks to a tall stock pot and cover with chicken stock. Add the onion, garlic, and sugar. Salt and pepper to taste. Bring to a rapid boil, then immediately reduce to medium heat and cover. Simmer until the hocks are tender and the meat pulls away from the bone, about 1 hour. Check the pot frequently to add more stock or water, as needed, to keep them submerged.

2. Proceed with Step 2 above.

IN A PINCH: When adding additional stock throughout this recipe, if you run out, use water. Don't stress, Shoog. Use what you have!

BRUNSWICK STEW

MAKES 16 SERVINGS

In the southeast, Brunswick Stew is a staple side dish at every barbecue restaurant. We eat it over fluffy white rice. This is Daddy's recipe—he taught me how to cook, after all. And for the love, please don't buy pulled pork at the grocery store. Support your local pit master or barbecue joint.

1 quart (4 cups) Rich Chicken Stock (64) or quality store-bought chicken stock

2 (14.5-ounce) cans diced tomatoes in juice

4 chicken breasts and 6 chicken thighs, bone-in and skin on

5 carrots, diced

5 medium potatoes, peeled and diced

2 yellow onions, chopped

1 (12-ounce) package thawed frozen baby lima beans

1 tsp salt, more as needed

1 tsp black pepper

½ tsp crushed red pepper flakes, optional

2 pounds pulled barbeque pork (the more marbled, the better)

1 (18-ounce) bottle hickory smoked barbecue sauce

1 (15.25-ounce) can whole kernel corn, drained

¼ cup cider vinegar

1 T light brown sugar

1 (6-ounce) can tomato paste

Cooked white rice, for serving

1. In a large Dutch oven, bring the stock and tomatoes with their juices to a boil over medium-high heat. Add the chicken. Cover and reduce heat to medium and simmer for 30 minutes, until chicken is tender. Remove chicken and allow to cool.

2. To the stock, add the carrots, potatoes, onions, beans, salt, black pepper, and crushed red pepper flakes, if using. Stir in the pulled pork, barbecue sauce, corn, vinegar, and brown sugar. Cover and simmer until the vegetables are tender, about 30 minutes.

3. Remove chicken from pot. Debone and shred chicken and return it to pot. Whisk in tomato paste to thicken. Cover and simmer another 5 to 10 minutes. Serve hot, over rice.

CHEF'S NOTE

The stew makes 4 quarts (16 cups), so you will want to freeze some. It can be cooled, transferred to covered containers, and refrigerated for up to 4 days or frozen in quart freezer bags for up to 3 months.

S
P

BUSY GIRL GREEN BEANS

MAKES 10 TO 12 SERVINGS

This is my go-to meal-prep side that doesn't taste like meal prep. It's super easy, keeps well in the fridge, and the portions are great for potlucks and hosting.

5 (14.5-ounce) cans cut green beans, preferably reduced-sodium, drained

3 T olive oil

1 T beef base concentrate, such as Better Than Bouillon

1 T garlic powder

½ tsp coarsely ground black pepper

1. Put the green beans, olive oil, beef concentrate, garlic powder, and black pepper in a large pot. Add enough water to cover the beans by 1 inch. Do not add salt!

2. Bring to a boil over high heat. Cook the beans without stirring for 20 to 25 minutes or until almost all the liquid has evaporated (set your timer and go do something productive). Be on standby toward the end to lightly stir the beans, making sure they don't burn. The texture is amazing. Serve hot.

The green beans can be cooled, covered, and refrigerated for up to 6 days in an airtight container.

GETCHYO' MAN GARDEN PEAS

MAKES 3 TO 4 SERVINGS

Growing up, we couldn't leave the dinner table until we'd finished all our vegetables. My nemesis was garden peas. I spent many lonely hours gagging over these thangs, until my Aunt Jackie fixed them for me this way. These pair well with my meatloaf, like Johnny and June (see "Ma, the Meatloaf!" 148). Double this recipe if cooking for more than two people.

1 (15-ounce) can LeSueur very young small sweet peas with mushrooms and pearl onions, with liquid

2 T salted butter

½ tsp garlic powder

½ tsp salt

½ tsp freshly ground black pepper

3 ounces cream cheese, cubed

1. In a small saucepan or pot, combine the peas (with their liquid), butter, garlic powder, salt, and black pepper. Bring to a boil over medium-high heat. Reduce the heat to medium-low and cover. Simmer until the peas are tender, about 12 minutes.

2. Turn off the heat and add the cream cheese to the pot. Let it stand for 1 to 2 minutes to soften. Carefully stir to melt the cream cheese, making sure all lumps are dissolved. The gravy will thicken as it sits. Serve hot.

SQUASH FRITTERS

MAKES 4 TO 6 SERVINGS

Growing up in the country, everybody planted a garden, so squash and zucchini were plentiful in the summertime. Stewed squash was a common side dish on our table. If your kids won't eat vegetables, squash fritters are a great way to break 'em in. My grandmother made these for us every summer with left-over stewed squash. Congratulations, you're about to get two recipes in one.

STEWED SQUASH

4 slices thick-cut bacon, chopped in 1-inch pieces

5 to 6 small yellow squash, sliced into ½-inch rounds

1 large Vidalia onion, sliced

Salt, to taste

Freshly ground black pepper, to taste

2 T salted butter, as needed

FRITTER BATTER

⅓ cup all-purpose flour

2 T yellow or white cornmeal

2 large eggs, lightly beaten

Neutral oil, for frying

Salt, to taste

1. **Make the stewed squash:** Line a plate with paper towels. Add the bacon to a large skillet over medium heat, stirring occasionally, until browned and crisp, about 7 to 8 minutes. Transfer the bacon to paper towels to drain, leaving the drippings in the skillet.

2. Add the squash to the pan and cook over medium heat, stirring occasionally, until tender, about 15 minutes. If the squash gives off a lot of juice, you may need to stew it in two batches so that it cooks faster and achieves the texture you want. Reserve that juice though. We won't waste it. Add the onion and season liberally with salt and pepper. Add a tablespoon or two of butter to prevent contents from sticking. Continue cooking until the vegetables are tender. Stir in the bacon. If making the stewed squash as a side dish, serve it immediately. If making fritters, transfer the squash to a medium bowl and let cool.

3. **Make the fritters:** Line a baking sheet with paper towels for draining the cooked fritters. Add the flour, cornmeal, and eggs to the the bowl of squash and mix well, making sure the eggs are absorbed. The mixture should be like a thick pancake batter, not soupy but not too stiff. If too thick, add a splash or two of the reserved cooking liquid so it's easy to spoon. If you don't have reserved cooking liquid, use water, stock, or milk as needed.

4. Pour enough oil to come about ¼ inch up the sides of a large skillet, and heat over medium-high until the oil is shimmering. Spoon a heaping tablespoon of the batter for each fritter into the hot oil, without overcrowding them. Fry, turning once, until golden brown, about 3

minutes on each side. Transfer the fritters to the paper towel–lined baking sheet. Sprinkle salt over the fritters and allow to cool a few minutes before serving.

CHEF'S NOTE

Using a nonstick pan to stew your squash will render more juices than cast iron. Drain off these juices and discard or freeze for yummy stock in gravies and soups. If using cast iron, you'll likely need to add more fat throughout the cooking process to prevent sticking.

EASY ROASTED VEGGIES

MAKES 4 SERVINGS

These thangs are addictive. It's a hearty side for a weekend dinner and for meal prep.

1 (12-ounce) bag fresh broccoli, cauliflower, and carrot medley

2 T olive oil

1 tsp garlic powder

1 tsp dried thyme, crushed

1 tsp salt

1 tsp freshly ground black pepper

1. Preheat the oven to 400°F. Line two large, rimmed baking sheets with parchment paper and set aside. Wash and cut the broccoli and cauliflower florets (longways) in halves or thirds. In a large bowl, add the veggies, oil, garlic powder, thyme, salt, and black pepper and toss to coat well. Spread onto the baking sheets, spacing the vegetables so the edges will get crispy. Do not overcrowd the pan.

2. Roast the vegetables for 10 to 12 minutes. Remove from the oven. Using a metal spatula, flip the vegetables and continue roasting until tender, about 10 more minutes. Serve hot.

PROPER GRITS

MAKES 4 TO 6 SERVINGS

There are two kinds of grits: proper grits and weak-ass grits. These nurse any hangover and make a heavenly bed for gravy. Do *not* add sugar. You're sweet enough.

2 cups water

¼ cup (½ stick) salted butter

½ tsp salt

1 cup quick (not instant) or old-fashioned stone-ground grits

1 cup half-and-half or heavy cream

1 cup Rich Chicken Stock (64) or store-bought stock

1 ½ cups (12 ounces) shredded sharp white cheddar

Salt, to taste

Freshly ground black pepper, to taste

1. In a medium saucepan, bring the water, butter, and salt to a boil over medium-high heat. Gradually whisk in the grits and bring to a boil, whisking often to avoid any lumps. Once the grits begin to bubble, reduce the heat to medium-low and gradually whisk in the cream and stock.

2. Reduce the heat to low and cover. Simmer for 20 to 30 minutes, stirring often to avoid grits sticking to the bottom of the pot. Allow more time for stone-ground grits. You can add more cream if the grits seem too thick.

3. Remove from the heat and whisk in the cheese. Taste before seasoning with salt and pepper. Serve hot.

CHEF'S NOTE

There is a 4-to-1 ratio of liquid to dry grits, so know that you have some leeway. If your grits sit too long before serving, they will thicken. To reheat, add a splash of milk or cream for desired consistency, and whisk continually over medium-low heat until heated through.

GETCHYO' MAN MACARONI CHEESE

MAKES 10 TO 12 SERVINGS

This recipe, passed down from my grandmother and Aunt JoAnn, is soul sister approved. If you're feelin' extra, substitute 2 heaping cups of Pimento Cheese (41) or Better-Than-Everybody's Buffalo Chicken Dip (42) for the Velveeta. You're dang welcome.

1 tsp garlic powder, divided

1 (16-ounce) box uncooked elbow pasta

8 ounces Velveeta, or other pasteurized cheese product

8 ounces (1 block) cream cheese

¼ cup (½ stick) salted butter, melted

2 (12-ounce) cans evaporated milk

4 large eggs

2 cups (16 ounces) shredded mozzarella, divided

2 cups (16 ounces) freshly shredded sharp cheddar, divided

1. Preheat the oven to 350°F. Bring a large saucepan pot of salted water to a boil over high heat, and add ½ teaspoon of garlic powder. Add the pasta and cook for 10 minutes. Meanwhile, cut the Velveeta and cream cheese into small cubes so they melt easily when you stir in the hot pasta. Add the Velveeta and cream cheese cubes to a large mixing bowl, along with the melted butter and remaining ½ teaspoon of garlic powder, and set aside.

2. Once pasta is done, drain it and add the hot pasta to the mixing bowl. Stir gently until the cheeses have melted and coated the pasta.

3. In a medium bowl, whisk the evaporated milk and eggs until combined and pour into the pasta mixture. Mix gently. Pour one half of the pasta mixture in a 9 x 13-inch baking dish. Sprinkle on 1 cup mozzarella and 1 cup cheddar. Pour on the remaining pasta mixture and top with the remaining mozzarella and cheddar.

4. Bake until the top is golden and bubbling, about 40 to 45 minutes. Serve hot.

SAVANNAH RED RICE

MAKES 6 TO 8 SERVINGS

My nana waited tables at Savannah's famous restaurant, The Pirates' House, in the 1960s. She often tells the story of a day when Martin Luther King Jr. and Ralph David Abernathy came in to eat lunch. It was 2:00 or 3:00 p.m., after the busy lunch rush, and none of the waitresses wanted to get up to serve them. "Well, they've gotta eat too," Nana exclaimed. MLK Jr. left her a twenty-dollar tip, one of the biggest tips she'd ever gotten. Here's my version of the restaurant's famous red rice recipe.

6 to 8 slices thick-cut bacon

1 small yellow onion, chopped

1 small green bell pepper, seeded and chopped

1 celery rib, chopped (½ cup)

Salt, to taste

Freshly ground black pepper, to taste

1 cup uncooked long-grain white rice

1 (14.5-ounce) can petite diced tomatoes with juice

1 ¾ cup Rich Chicken Stock (64) or store-bought chicken stock, as needed

2 tsp sugar

1 tsp salt

⅛ tsp cayenne pepper

1. Line a plate with paper towels. Heat a medium skillet over medium heat. Cook the bacon until crisp and browned, about 7 to 8 minutes. Transfer the bacon to paper towels to drain, reserving 2 to 3 tablespoons of drippings. Crumble the bacon once it cools.

2. Pour the reserved bacon drippings into a medium saucepan or pot and heat over medium heat. Add the onion, green pepper, celery, salt, and black pepper and cook, until softened, about 7 to 9 minutes. Add the crumbled bacon and the uncooked rice. Stir to toast the rice (to get it acquainted with everything in the pan). Stir in the tomatoes and their juices. Fill the tomato can to the brim with stock or water, and add it to the pot. Add the sugar, salt, and cayenne (pot should be boiling). Cover and reduce to a simmer over low heat for 20 minutes.

3. Remove the rice from the heat. Fluff with a fork and serve.

SQUASH CASSEROLE

MAKES 8 TO 10 SERVINGS

We had *really* good school lunches growing up in Effingham County, Georgia. I'd feed my high school's squash casserole to Chef Sean Brock. Here's my rendition.

4 to 6 slices bacon

5 to 6 small yellow squash, sliced ½-inch thick rounds

1 medium Vidalia onion, chopped

1 small red bell pepper, seeded and chopped

Salt, to taste

Freshly ground black pepper, to taste

1 to 2 T butter, as needed

1 (12-ounce) bag herb stuffing mix, such as Pepperidge Farm (the blue bag), divided

1 ½ cups From-Scratch Cream of Chicken Soup (67), or store-bought

1 cup freshly shredded sharp cheddar

½ cup (1 stick) salted butter, melted

¾ cup grated carrots

1 cup (8 ounces) sour cream

2 eggs, beaten

1. Preheat the oven to 350°F. Lightly butter a 9 x 13-inch baking dish. Heat a large skillet over medium heat. Add the bacon and cook until crisp and browned, about 7 to 8 minutes. Transfer the bacon to paper towels to drain, leaving the drippings in the skillet. Crumble the bacon once it cools.

2. Add the squash and cook over medium heat, stirring occasionally, until it's partially tender, about 8 minutes. If the squash gives off a lot of juice, tilt the pan and spoon the liquid into a coffee cup to reserve. (If the squash is giving off a lot of juice, you may be overcrowding your pan and need to cook this in 2 batches.) Add the onion and bell pepper and season with salt and pepper, to taste. Add a tablespoon or 2 of butter, as needed, to keep the contents from sticking. Continue cooking until the vegetables are tender, about 5 to 10 minutes. Salt and pepper to taste, then transfer to a large mixing bowl.

3. Reserve ⅔ cup stuffing mix and set aside. To the large mixing bowl add the crumbled bacon, remaining stuffing mix, soup, cheese, melted butter, carrots, sour cream, and eggs. Mix until combined and season with salt and pepper. Spread into the baking dish, top with remaining stuffing mix, and bake about 30 minutes. Serve hot.

CHEF'S NOTE

Small squash are about the length of your hand. As squash grow larger, they becomes tough and seedy. If using mature squash, increase the cook time and reduce the amount of squash used.

P

YOU AIN'T NEVUH HAD THESE BLACK-EYED PEAS

MAKES 10 TO 12 SERVINGS

Don't serve canned black-eyed peas. We're not animals. Plan your meals ahead of time, like the classy host(ess) you were born to be. Make sure to soak the peas overnight. All you'll have to do is fix a pan of cornbread 20 minutes before mealtime.

1 bag (16 ounces) dried black-eyed peas

½ tsp baking soda, optional (see Chef's Note)

2 to 3 ham hocks

2 garlic cloves, minced

1 large yellow onion, diced, divided

½ tsp salt

½ tsp freshly ground black pepper

3 T granulated sugar, divided

4 cups Rich Chicken Stock (64), or unsalted store-bought chicken stock

1 jalapeño pepper, seeded chopped

1 T cider vinegar

Hot sauce, to taste, preferably Texas Pete or Louisiana Hot Sauce

2 to 3 sprigs fresh thyme

Salt, to taste

Freshly ground black pepper, to taste

Raw onion, diced, for serving

1. In a large Crock-Pot or stock pot, add the dried black-eyed peas and cover with water so that the water rises 3 inches above the peas. Add baking soda, if using. Soak for at least 14 hours or overnight.

2. In a small stock pot, add the ham hocks, garlic, ½ of the onion, salt, pepper, and 1 tablespoon of sugar. Cover with chicken stock and enough water so the liquid sits 2 to 3 inches above the hocks. Bring to a boil. Reduce to a medium heat and cook until hocks are fork-tender, about 1 hour. Add more stock as needed throughout the cooking process to keep the hocks submerged. The liquid will condense and darken in color. This is liquid gold.

3. While the hocks cook, drain and rinse your peas and return them to a large Crock-Pot. Add remaining ½ of the onion, remaining 2 tablespoons of sugar, jalapeño, vinegar, and hot sauce. Add the hocks and their stock. Stir gently and top with thyme. Season with salt and pepper, to taste. Cover Crock-Pot

and cook on high for about 3 to 4 hours. Or cook on low for about 8 to 10 hours.

4. Mash a small portion of the peas with a spoon to thicken the pot liquor, as desired. Stir and serve with diced raw onion and Buttermilk Cornbread (71).

IN A PINCH: When adding additional stock throughout this recipe, if you run out, use water. Don't stress, honey. Use what you've got!

CHEF'S NOTE

Mama always adds baking soda when soaking her beans because it can help reduce gas. (Your boo will thank me later.)

Sauces and More

dio-technica
BALANCE
VOLUME
MAX
LOUDNESS
TAPE MONITOR
1 2
FUNCTION
AM FM PHONO
AUX/MIC
MIC
AM 55 60 70 80 90 110 140 160
FM 88 90 92 94 96 98 100 102 105 108

GRANDMA'S 14-DAY SWEET PICKLES

BODACIOUS TOMATO GRAVY

HANTAH'S BARBECUE SAUCE

HONEY MUSTARD

TARTAR SAUCE

CROCK-POT APPLE BUTTER

CHOCOLATE GRAVY

BETTER THAN WHIPPED CREAM

GRANDMA'S 14-DAY SWEET PICKLES

MAKES APPROXIMATELY 4 GALLONS

DO NOT SLEEP ON THESE! They're the secret to my pasta, chicken, potato salad, and more. These make great gifts, and you will go through them quicker than you think. The process of making these takes a while, so plan ahead. Turn it into a bonding experience with a loved one. Kumbaya.

BRINE

16 pounds Kirby pickling cucumbers

2 cups non-iodized salt (Kosher salt, sea salt, or canning and pickling salt)

1 gallon water

PICKLING

1 (1.9-ounce) packet alum powder

2 cups warm water, plus more cool water

2 gallons cider vinegar

2 (1.5-ounce) containers pickling spice mix

1 (10-pound) bag sugar

SUPPLIES

5-gallon food-safe bucket or ceramic crock

Dinner plate to fit inside the bucket

Four pieces of cheesecloth

Kitchen twine

Glass canning jars with lids and rings (you don't have to hot-water process these pickles—hallelujah!)

1. **Brine the cucumbers:** Scrub the cucumbers well and pack them in a 5-gallon bucket or ceramic crock. Dissolve the salt in 1 gallon of water and pour over the cucumbers. Put a dinner plate over the cucumbers and weigh down the plate to keep the cucumbers submerged. Cover the bucket with a cheese cloth or towel. Soak for 14 days in this same brine in a cool, dark place.

2. **Pickle the cucumbers:** On the fourteenth day, drain the cucumbers and rinse under cold water to remove any white film, as needed. Wash and dry the bucket.

3. Cut the cucumbers into desired pieces and return to the cleaned bucket. Dissolve the alum in warm water and pour over cucumber pieces. Add more (cool) water to the bucket to just cover the cucumbers, and once more place a dinner plate over the cucumbers to keep them submerged. Cover with a cheesecloth or towel and let stand overnight.

4. The next morning, drain, rinse, and cover the cucumbers with vinegar, as needed (you might not need 2 full gallons). Again, place a dinner plate over the cucumbers to ensure they are submerged, cover the bucket with a towel, and let stand for 6 hours.

5. After 6 hours, pour cucumbers and vinegar into a clean kitchen sink, allowing the vinegar to drain. Evenly distribute the pickling spices into 4 cheesecloths and tie closed with kitchen twine.

6. Put one-fourth of the pickles into the cleaned bucket. Top with a spice packet and cover with 2 ½ pounds (about 5 ⅔ cups) of sugar. Repeat this process 3 more times (pickles, spice packet, sugar). Cover the bucket with a towel and let stand 3 to 5 days in a cool, dark place. This will allow the syrup to form.

7. Sterilize glass jars and lids by placing them in boiling water. Remove with tongs, and allow them to air dry. Use whatever jars you have on hand! Pint and quart jars are great for gifting. You can store any extra pickles in plastic containers in your fridge. Tightly pack the pickles and their syrup into sterilized jars, being sure the pickles are covered with syrup. Wipe the rims clean with a moist paper towel and add the lids and rings.

Store in the fridge or a cool, dark place for up to 1 year. Refrigerate after opening.

Gravy Is Easy

Gravy should be flavorful and thick. You need only a few ingredients to make good gravy, and you're always gonna have 'em on hand . . . if you're paying attention. The stock should match the animal fat, and the gravy should match the dish. For example, if you're serving chicken, make chicken gravy using chicken fat and chicken stock. Here's the trick: Use three parts each of fat, flour, and liquid—easy!

3 T fat

3 T flour

3 cups liquid

1. In a large skillet melt a few tablespoons of that animal fat I told ya to save over medium-low heat (bacon grease works in a pinch).

2. Reduce heat to low, sprinkle in your flour, and stir to combine. Note: If your skillet isn't well-seasoned, it'll absorb some of the fat. In this case, you'll need to add another tablespoon of fat or butter.

3. Once the flour takes on some color, add your liquid. Cold liquid works best, but don't sweat it. Whisk it until smooth.

4. Doctor up your gravy with ½ teaspoon each of garlic powder, onion powder, sugar, and bouillon (optional). I go heavy on the pepper. Simmer on medium-low for a few minutes to thicken. Season to taste, and serve over some heavenly carbohydrate.

BODACIOUS TOMATO GRAVY

MAKES ABOUT 1 QUART

Everybody has their own idea of what tomato gravy is. They ain't wrong. My idea ain't wrong either. Serve it up over rice, biscuits, or pasta.

6 slices thick-cut bacon

½ medium sweet onion, finely chopped

3 heaping T flour

1 (28-ounce) can crushed tomatoes

1 tsp salt

½ tsp freshly ground black pepper

½ tsp garlic powder

2 heaping T brown sugar

¼ cup heavy cream

1. Heat a large skillet (preferably cast iron) over medium heat. When it's hot, add the bacon and cook until brown and crispy, about 7 to 8 minutes. Reduce the heat to medium-low and transfer the bacon to a paper towel–lined plate to drain. Reserve about 3 tablespoons of drippings in the skillet.

2. Add the onion to the drippings and cook until tender, about 5 minutes. Sprinkle in the flour and stir to coat the grease. Cook until the flour is lightly browned in color, about 2 minutes. Add the tomatoes and stir. Add the salt, black pepper, garlic powder, and brown sugar. Simmer to thicken, about 5 minutes. Stir in the cream and turn off the heat. Crumble the bacon and sprinkle on top of the gravy. Serve hot.

The gravy can be cooled, covered, and refrigerated for up to 3 days.

HANTAH'S BARBECUE SAUCE

MAKES ABOUT 2 CUPS

Baptize your pork in this. Daddy taught me to marry Carolina Gold with red, tangy vinegar sauce. Here's my recipe.

1 cup cider vinegar

1 cup packed brown sugar

1 cup ketchup

2 T chili powder

4 T cane syrup or molasses

4 T yellow mustard

2 tsp smoked paprika

2 tsp garlic powder

2 tsp salt

2 tsp coarsely ground black pepper

½ tsp cayenne pepper

½ tsp ground cumin

1. In a small saucepan or pot, stir the vinegar and brown sugar over medium heat until the sugar dissolves. Let stand for 20 to 30 minutes to cool.

2. Pour the sweetened vinegar into a quart-sized glass canning jar. Add the ketchup, chili powder, cane syrup (or molasses), mustard, paprika, garlic powder, salt, black pepper, cayenne, and cumin. Cover and shake the stew out of it.

The sauce can be refrigerated for up to 2 weeks.

HONEY MUSTARD

MAKES ABOUT 1/2 CUP

This'll make ya say, "Hunny, hush" (in your best Jerry Reed voice).

2 T yellow mustard

2 T mayonnaise

2 T buttermilk

3 T honey

1/8 tsp garlic powder

Pinch of sweet paprika

Make it in this order or it'll be lumpy: Whisk the mustard and mayonnaise together in a small bowl until smooth. Add the buttermilk and whisk until smooth. Add the honey, garlic powder, and paprika and whisk well. Cover and refrigerate until ready to use.

The honey mustard can be refrigerated for up to 2 weeks.

TARTAR SAUCE

MAKES ABOUT 1 CUP

Put this on fish, seafood, hush puppies, fried potatoes, chicken fingers . . . it's even good on a hotdog. Trust me.

Heaping ⅓ cup mayonnaise, preferably Blue Plate

¼ cup sweet onion, such as Vidalia, finely chopped

3 T dill pickles, chopped, or dill relish, drained

1 T white vinegar

1 tsp sugar, as needed

¼ tsp freshly ground black pepper

Whisk the mayonnaise, onion, pickles, vinegar, sugar, and pepper in a small bowl or a cute little Tupperware container. Cover and refrigerate until ready to serve. This is great with fresh dill and some drained, chopped capers too. Use what you have, Carol!

The tartar sauce can be refrigerated for up to 5 days.

CROCK-POT APPLE BUTTER

MAKES 7 TO 8 HALF-PINT JARS

This is the best I've eaten—even if it is my own recipe. This stuff was made for Cathead Biscuits (72), Cinnamon Apple Beer Bread (79), and so much more!

3 ½ pounds Honeycrisp apples, peeled, cored, and cut into ⅓-inch wedges

3 pounds Granny Smith apples, peeled, cored, and cut into ⅓-inch wedges

1 ½ cups granulated sugar

1 cup packed dark brown sugar

1 T ground cinnamon

½ tsp salt

½ tsp ground nutmeg

Scant ¼ tsp ground cloves

2 T fresh lemon juice

1 ½ tsp vanilla extract

1. Put the apples in a large (7 to 8-quart) Crock-Pot. In a separate bowl, whisk the sugar, brown sugar, cinnamon, salt, nutmeg, and cloves, and pour over the apples. Cover and cook on high for 5 hours.

2. Stir in the lemon juice and vanilla and cook on low, uncovered, for 2 hours more. Allow the apple butter to cool. Emulsify with an immersion blender just until smooth (use a blender if you don't have an immersion blender). Don't overdo this part. You want it to remain thick.

3. Pour into 7 to 8 freezer-safe half-pint jars. Wipe the rims clean and cover with the lids and rings.

The apple butter can be refrigerated for 2 to 3 weeks or frozen for about 1 year. Thaw frozen apple butter at room temperature for about 10 minutes before using. I water-bath can mine to save room in the freezer. Reference my TikTok for videos on canning.

CHOCOLATE GRAVY

MAKES ABOUT 1 1/2 CUPS, 4 TO 6 SERVINGS

I'd never heard of chocolate gravy until I moved to Nashville. My Mississippi and Alabama friends raved about it. Now I know why . . . here's my version.

- ⅓ cup sugar
- 2 to 3 T all-purpose flour
- 3 T cocoa, preferably Dutch-processed (see Chef's Note)
- ⅛ teaspoon instant coffee
- Pinch of salt
- 1 ½ cups whole milk
- 2 T butter
- 1 tsp vanilla extract

In a medium skillet over medium heat, whisk the sugar, flour, cocoa, coffee, and salt, about 2 to 3 minutes, until heated. Gradually whisk in the milk and bring to a simmer. When it starts to bubble and thicken, whisk in the butter and turn off the heat. Stir in the vanilla. Serve immediately. Cover and refrigerate any leftovers for up to 3 days. Reheat if you want it to be gravy again or just eat it cold like I do. Yum!

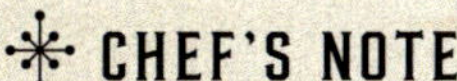

CHEF'S NOTE

Dutch-processed cocoa makes a darker, richer gravy, but you can use regular cocoa too. Serve on biscuits or your boyfriend.

BETTER THAN WHIPPED CREAM

MAKES ABOUT 3 CUPS

Better than Cool Whip, Brenda. You're welcome.

1 ½ cups heavy cream

1 tsp clear vanilla extract

2 T powdered sugar

Pinch of salt

1. In a chilled medium bowl, beat the heavy cream, vanilla, powdered sugar, and salt.

2. For stiff peaks, use a medium speed for about 5 to 7 minutes until the tips of the whipped cream stand upright and firm. Do not overmix, or the mixture will curdle. Serve immediately.

Desserts

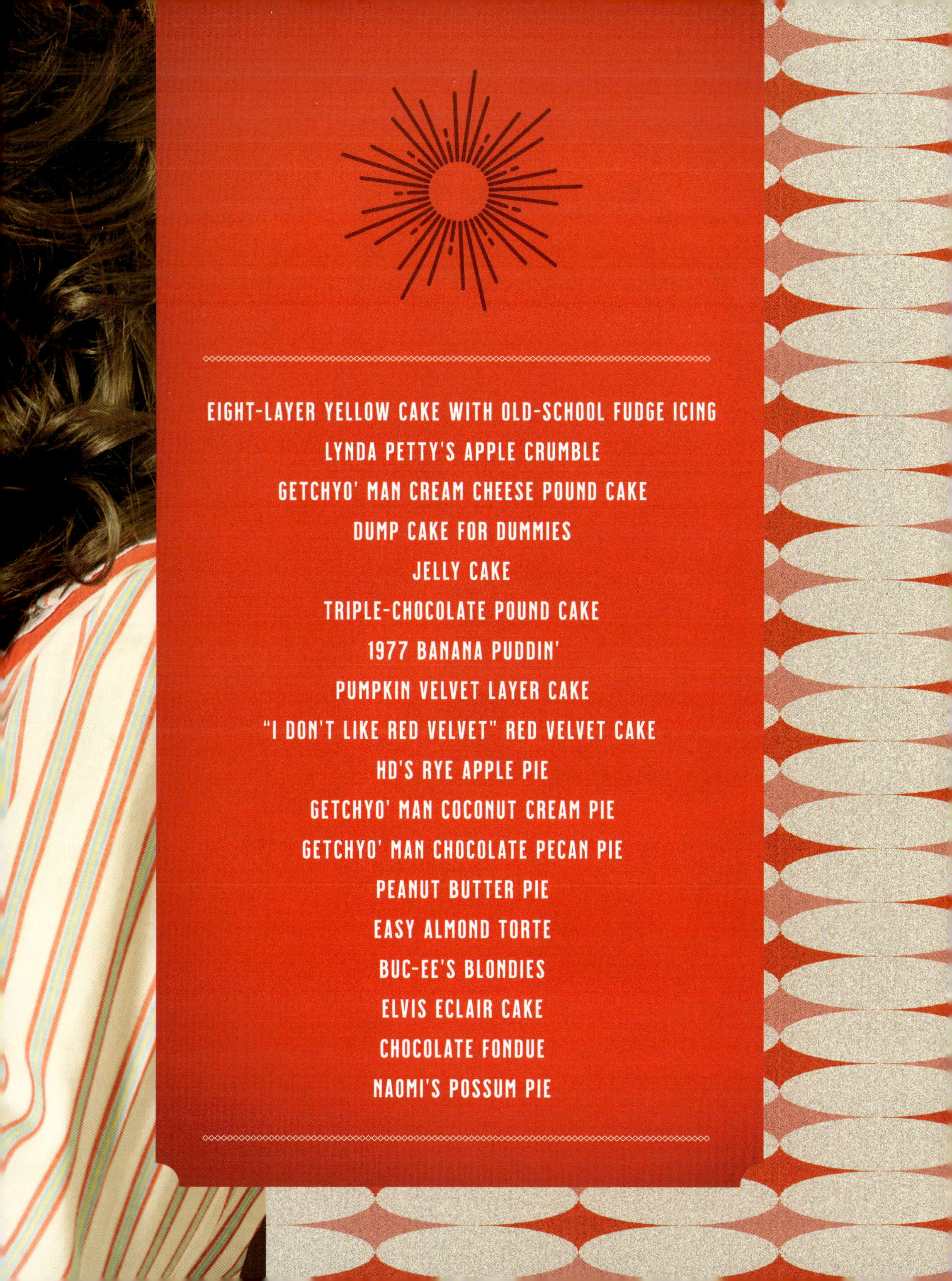
EIGHT-LAYER YELLOW CAKE WITH OLD-SCHOOL FUDGE ICING
LYNDA PETTY'S APPLE CRUMBLE
GETCHYO' MAN CREAM CHEESE POUND CAKE
DUMP CAKE FOR DUMMIES
JELLY CAKE
TRIPLE-CHOCOLATE POUND CAKE
1977 BANANA PUDDIN'
PUMPKIN VELVET LAYER CAKE
"I DON'T LIKE RED VELVET" RED VELVET CAKE
HD'S RYE APPLE PIE
GETCHYO' MAN COCONUT CREAM PIE
GETCHYO' MAN CHOCOLATE PECAN PIE
PEANUT BUTTER PIE
EASY ALMOND TORTE
BUC-EE'S BLONDIES
ELVIS ECLAIR CAKE
CHOCOLATE FONDUE
NAOMI'S POSSUM PIE

EIGHT-LAYER YELLOW CAKE WITH OLD-SCHOOL FUDGE ICING

MAKES 12 TO 14 SERVINGS

Divorce your yellow boxed cake. I'm about to take you to texture town . . . Down South, cakes like this—stacked 8 to 14 layers high—were reserved for special occasions. You hired someone to make them, unless you were lucky enough to have a relative who knew how to make one—and still would.

Picture thin layers of fluffy homemade yellow cake, sandwiched between the most decadent old-school chocolate fudge icing. Silky and shining from the sugar crystals, this cake is a moment. I spent a lot of time writing and perfecting this recipe, so enjoy it, Shoog! Don't skip the butter flavoring.

CAKE

Softened butter and flour, for the pans

1 ½ cups sugar

⅓ cup butter-flavored vegetable shortening, such as Crisco, cut into tablespoons

5 T salted butter, softened, cut into tablespoons

2 large eggs plus 2 large egg whites, beaten together

2 cups all-purpose flour, sifted, preferably White Lily

2 tsp baking powder

1 tsp cornstarch

1 tsp salt

½ cup half-and-half

1 tsp butter flavoring

½ tsp vanilla extract

½ cup sour cream

FUDGE ICING

1 cup (2 sticks) unsalted butter

¼ cup unsweetened cocoa powder

2 ½ cups granulated sugar

¾ cup half-and-half or evaporated milk

1 T light corn syrup, such as Karo

¼ tsp salt

2 ¼ cups mini marshmallows

1 tsp vanilla extract

1. **Bake the cake layers:** Preheat the oven to 350°F. Liberally butter and flour 8 (8-inch) cake pans and tap out the excess flour (buy 8 disposable aluminum pans for easy cleanup, or bake in shifts if you have only 2 or 3 pans).

2. In a large bowl, cream together the sugar, shortening, and butter with a mixer until fluffy (about 3 minutes). Add the eggs and egg whites. Mix well.

3. In a separate bowl, sift together the flour, baking powder, cornstarch, and salt. Add your flour mixture to the batter, along with the half-and-half, butter flavoring, and vanilla. Mix on medium speed, just until the batter is moistened, about 15 seconds. Scrape down the sides of the bowl and mix just until the batter is smooth, about 10 seconds more. Do not overmix. Fold in the sour cream. Spoon the batter evenly into the 8 cake pans. The batter will be thin, less than ¼-inch thick in each pan.

4. Bake the cakes in multiple batches to prevent overcrowding the oven. Space the cake pans evenly on the racks (about two inches apart), and bake about 5 to 6 minutes, or until the cakes barely shrink from the sides of the pan. Transfer the pans to wire cooling racks and let cool for 5 to 10 minutes. Run a knife around the inside of each pan and unmold each layer onto the racks to cool completely.

5. **Make the fudge icing:** In a medium saucepan or pot over low heat, melt the butter and cocoa and whisk constantly until little bubbles form.

6. Whisk in the sugar, half-and-half (or evaporated milk), corn syrup, and salt. Increase the heat to medium-high, whisking continually until the mixture begins to boil. Immediately set a timer for 3 minutes. After 2 minutes have passed, turn off the burner. Leave the pot on the burner for the remaining 1 minute. Once the timer goes off, remove from the heat.

7. Quickly whisk in the marshmallows until they have dissolved. Continue to whisk for 1 minute. Allow the icing to cool for 3 minutes to thicken slightly (it should still be very warm and pourable but thick enough to adhere to the cake). Whisk in the vanilla, then move quickly to frost the cake.

8. **Assemble the cake:** Place a cake layer on a cake platter. Ladle about ⅓ cup of icing over the first layer. Spread the icing to the edges with a knife (you want the icing layers to be thin so you have enough fudge leftover to cover the top and sides of the cake). Repeat with the remaining layers. As excess icing gathers at the bottom of the plate, use your knife to pull it up the sides of the cake while it's still pliable. If the layers slide, stick them in place with long wooden skewer toothpicks. Pour the remaining icing over the top of the cake, and allow it to drip down the sides. Smooth the edges to cover completely. If the icing becomes too stiff, melt it a little in the saucepan over low heat and whisk until smooth.

9. Let the cake stand for an hour before cutting to set the icing.

The cake can be stored under a cake dome at room temperature for up to 5 days.

CHEF'S NOTE

If you use too much icing between your layers and run out before you're able to frost the outsides of the cake, don't fret. Just make an additional half batch.

FOR A SHEET CAKE: Butter and flour a 9 x 13-inch baking dish and bake for 25 to 30 minutes. Transfer the pan to a wire cooling rack to cool. Cover the top with the icing. Lots of it.

FROM-SCRATCH RED VELVET CAKE: Substitute 1/4 cup unsweetened cocoa powder for an equal amount of all-purpose flour. Add one 1-ounce bottle of red food coloring with the eggs and whites.

LYNDA PETTY'S APPLE CRUMBLE

MAKES 6 TO 8 SERVINGS

On occasion, you can catch me singin' the anthem at a NASCAR race. My sweet friend Montgomery (granddaughter of NASCAR legend, Richard Petty) shared this recipe with me. It was handwritten by her Mimi, the late Lynda Petty, on the cutest retro strawberry index card. Here's that recipe with my homemade pie filling. I now use this recipe for all my fruit crumbles.

3 cups apple pie filling (238)

1 ¾ cup sugar, divided

1 cup all-purpose flour

1 tsp baking soda

1 egg

½ cup (1 stick)
salted butter, melted

1. Preheat the oven to 375°F. Pour the pie filling in a 9 x 9-inch baking dish or deep-dish pie pan. Sprinkle ¾ cup sugar on top (optional).

2. Whisk the flour, remaining 1 cup sugar, and baking soda in a medium bowl. Add the egg and mix with a fork until crumbly. Sprinkle over the filling. Pour the melted butter on top.

3. Bake until the topping is golden brown and the juices are bubbling, about 45 minutes. Serve warm.

GETCHYO' MAN CREAM CHEESE POUND CAKE

MAKES 12 SERVINGS

Some pound cakes are so dry they'll make ya poot dust. Not this one! Mama makes a mean one. This is my version of her recipe. Make sure you use cake flour, and don't beat the hell out of it.

Softened butter and sugar, to prepare the pan

1 ½ cups (3 sticks) salted butter, softened

8 ounces (1 block) cream cheese, softened

3 ¼ cups sugar

3 cups cake flour, such as Swans Down, divided

¼ tsp salt

6 large eggs, room temperature

1 tsp vanilla extract

1 tsp almond extract

1. Preheat the oven to 315°F. Liberally butter the inside of a nonstick Bundt pan. Be sure to get into every crevice. Dust the inside liberally with sugar, and tap out the excess.

2. In a large bowl, using an electric mixer on high speed, beat the butter and cream cheese until combined, about 1 minute. Add the sugar and mix until light and fluffy (about 4 minutes), scraping down the bowl as needed with a silicone spatula.

3. Add 1 cup of the cake flour, salt, and 2 eggs, and mix just until the yolks disappear into the batter, about 8 to 10 seconds (I just pulse my mixer so as not to overbeat it). Scrape the sides and bottom of the bowl, and repeat with another 1 cup of cake flour and 2 eggs. Pulse to mix. Scrape and repeat with the remaining cake flour and eggs, this time adding the vanilla and almond extracts. Mix until the batter is smooth, about 8 seconds. Again, do not overmix. Scrape the batter into the prepared pan, and tap the pan on the counter to release any bubbles. Pray over it.

4. Bake the cake until golden brown, about 1 hour and 15 minutes. Let cool on a wire rack for 15 minutes. Unmold the cake onto a plate, and let it cool completely before cutting.

The cake can be wrapped in plastic wrap and stored at room temperature for up to 5 days. Stale cake makes great French toast and shortcake too.

IN A DASH: Stick the eggs in your bra to bring them to room temperature faster.

DUMP CAKE FOR DUMMIES

MAKES 12 SERVINGS

For the love—don't show up to a gathering empty-handed. This is my most viral recipe. It's called a "dump cake" because you can literally dump everything into one mixing bowl. Now that you own the book, here's the way I *really* make it at home. Easy!

Softened butter and flour, to prepare the pan, or nonstick cooking spray

1 (15.25-ounce) box yellow cake mix, such as Duncan Hines

1 (3.4-ounce) package instant vanilla pudding mix

1 T baking powder

2 cups semisweet chocolate chips

4 large eggs

½ cup neutral oil

½ cup whole milk

1 cup sour cream

½ tsp butter flavoring

Powdered sugar, for garnish

1. Preheat oven to 350°F. Liberally grease a Bundt pan or use nonstick cooking spray, being sure to get into every crevice. Dust the inside with flour and tap out the excess.
2. In a large bowl, whisk together the cake mix, pudding mix, and baking powder. Add the chocolate chips and toss to coat them. In a separate bowl, whisk the eggs, oil, milk, sour cream, and butter flavoring. Pour the wet mixture into the dry ingredients and mix with a whisk, just until combined. Do not overmix. Scrape the batter into the prepared pan and smooth the top. Lick the spoon.
3. Bake the cake about 45 to 50 minutes. Let cool on a wire rack for 15 minutes. Unmold the cake onto a plate and let cool completely. Texture town.
4. Just before serving, sift powdered sugar over the top to make it look like you did somethin', Cheryl.

The cake can be wrapped in plastic wrap or stored in a cake keeper at room temperature for up to 5 days.

CHEF'S NOTE

CHOCOLATE LOVER'S VERSION: Make the batter using chocolate pudding mix instead of vanilla, and substitute strong brewed coffee for the milk.

JELLY CAKE

MAKES 12 TO 14 SERVINGS

When Papa quit drinkin', he had a powerful sweet tooth. You could always find a jelly cake—or part of one—sitting on the counter at their house.

2 ½ (13-ounce) jars blackberry jelly

1 ¼ cups (2 ½ sticks) salted butter, melted

Eight-Layer Yellow Cake (219), without frosting

Better Than Whipped Cream (213) or vanilla ice cream (optional)

1. In a medium bowl, whisk the jelly and butter together until combined.

2. Spread about one-eighth of the filling over the warm cake, letting the filling run down the sides. Repeat with the remaining layers. If the layers slide, stick them in place with long wooden skewers or toothpicks and remove once filling sets. Let stand until the filling sets, about 1 hour. Slice and serve with a large dollop of sweetened whipped cream, not the fake stuff.

The cake can be stored under a cake dome at room temperature for up to 3 days.

TRIPLE-CHOCOLATE POUND CAKE

MAKES 12 SERVINGS

Humbly, this is the best pound cake I've ever had. Chocolatey and rich like Kevin Hart.

POUND CAKE

Softened butter and sugar, to prepare the pan

1 ½ cups (3 sticks) salted butter, softened

8 ounces (1 block) cream cheese, softened

½ tsp salt

3 ¼ cups sugar

2 ½ cups plus 1 T cake flour, such as Swans Down, divided

6 large eggs, room temperature

½ cup unsweetened cocoa powder, preferably Hershey's Special Dark

1 tsp vanilla extract

1 tsp almond extract

1 T strong coffee, cold, or ¼ tsp instant coffee

2 cups semisweet chocolate chips

GLAZE

6 T salted butter, cut up

1 cup semisweet chocolate chips

1. **Make the pound cake:** Preheat the oven to 315°F. Liberally butter the inside of a nonstick Bundt pan, being sure to get into every crevice. Dust the inside liberally with sugar and tap out the excess.

2. In a large bowl, beat the butter and cream cheese with an electric mixer on high speed for about 1 minute (scrape down the sides of the bowl with a spatula to ensure that everything is incorporated). Add the salt and sugar, and mix until light and fluffy, about 4 minutes. Add 1 cup of cake flour and 2 eggs, and mix just until the yolks disappear into the batter, about 10 seconds (I pulse my mixer so as not to overbeat it). Scrape the sides and bottom of the bowl, and repeat with another 1 cup of cake flour and 2 eggs. Pulse to mix. Scrape and repeat with the remaining ½ cup of cake flour and the cocoa and 2 eggs, this time adding the vanilla extract, almond extract, and coffee. Mix about 8 seconds more, just until the batter is smooth. Again, do not overmix.

3. In a small bowl, toss the chocolate chips with the remaining 1 tablespoon cake flour to coat. Fold this into the batter. Scrape into the prepared pan and smooth the top of the batter to evenly distribute.

4. Bake the cake about 1 hour and 15 minutes. Let cool on a wire rack for 15 minutes. The cake will set as it cools. Invert and unmold the cake onto a cake plate, and let cool completely.

5. **Make the glaze:** In a small microwave-safe bowl, melt the butter and chocolate chips in

30-second intervals (no more than 90 seconds total). Whisk until smooth and pour over cooled cake. Make more if desired.

The cake can be stored in a cake keeper at room temperature for up to 5 days.

1977 BANANA PUDDIN'

MAKES 8 TO 10 SERVINGS

Nashville 1977: It was the year Elvis died, Skynyrd's plane crashed, and *Smokey and the Bandit*, my favorite film of all time, was the highest-grossing film at the box office. Meanwhile, Tammy Wynette was having a date night at home with her new boyfriend, Burt Reynolds. She nearly sent the movie star into a diabetic coma when she served him her famous banana puddin'. (True story. He passed out on her couch. She didn't realize he was hypoglycemic.) This is my version of that recipe, but I add sour cream to make it richer. Stand by Your Insulin.

FROM-SCRATCH VANILLA PUDDING

1 (11-ounce) box vanilla wafers, crushed, divided

2 cups sugar

1 cup self-rising flour

Pinch of salt

6 large egg yolks

5 cups whole milk

1 tsp vanilla extract

1 cup sour cream

6 ripe bananas, sliced

MERINGUE

6 large egg whites, at room temperature (just let them sit out while making the pudding)

½ cup sugar

1. Preheat the oven to 350°F. Spread half of the crushed vanilla wafers to cover the bottom of a 9 x 13-inch baking dish. Reserve the remaining wafers.

2. **Make the pudding:** In a large heavy saucepan or pot, whisk the sugar with the flour and salt. Add the egg yolks. Do not whisk the egg yolks yet or the mixture will be lumpy. Add 2 cups of milk, then begin whisking as you gradually add the remaining milk. Cook over medium heat, whisking constantly, until the pudding begins to bubble and thicken, about 5 to 7 minutes. Remove from the heat and whisk in the vanilla. Let cool to room temperature. Fold the sour cream into the cooled pudding mixture.

3. In the baking dish, spread the sliced bananas evenly over the vanilla wafers and pour the pudding over the top. Sprinkle the reserved wafers over the pudding.

4. **Make the meringue:** In a medium bowl, with an electric mixer on high beat the egg whites until they form soft peaks. With the mixer running, gradually beat in the sugar to make a meringue with stiff and shiny peaks. Spread the meringue evenly over the top layer, being sure it touches the sides of the dish. Make it look pretty.

5. Bake the pudding until the meringue tips are golden brown, about 8 to 10 minutes. Serve immediately or chill for 3 to 4 hours. The pudding can be refrigerated for up to 3 days.

PUMPKIN VELVET LAYER CAKE

MAKES 12 SERVINGS

Let's doctor up a cake mix, Debbie. We've got rockstar thangs to do.

PUMPKIN VELVET CAKE

Softened butter and flour, to prepare the pan

1 (15.25-ounce) box yellow cake mix, such as Duncan Hines

1 (3.4-ounce) small box instant vanilla or pumpkin spice pudding mix

1 T pumpkin pie spice

¼ tsp salt

1 cup canned 100% pure pumpkin

4 large eggs

½ cup peanut oil or butter, melted (or butter-flavored Crisco, melted)

½ cup whole milk

½ cup sour cream

CREAM CHEESE ICING

12 ounces (1 ½ blocks) cream cheese, softened

½ cup (1 stick) butter, softened

2 tsp vanilla extract

Pinch of salt

8 to 10 cups powdered sugar, plus more as needed

Pecan halves, toasted, for garnish (optional)

1. **Make the cake:** Preheat the oven to 350°F. Butter 3 (8-inch) round cake pans and dust with flour.

2. In a large bowl, whisk the cake mix, pudding mix, pumpkin pie spice, and salt. In a separate bowl, whisk the pumpkin, eggs, oil, milk, and sour cream to combine. Fold the wet mixture into the dry ingredients and mix by hand or with an electric mixer on medium speed just until combined. Do not overmix. Divide evenly among the prepared pans and smooth the tops.

3. Bake the cakes, spacing the cake pans evenly on the oven rack (don't let them touch), for about 15 minutes, or until the cakes barely shrink from the sides of the pan. Let cool on a wire rack for 15 minutes. Unmold the cakes onto parchment and place on wire cooling racks for 15 to 20 minutes.

4. **Make the icing:** In a large bowl, beat the cream cheese and butter on high speed with an electric mixer until smooth. Beat in the vanilla and salt. Reduce to a low speed and gradually beat in the powdered sugar to make a smooth, spreadable icing. Increase the speed to high and continue beating until fluffy, about 2 minutes more. Add more powdered sugar if the icing seems too thin.

5. **Frost the cake:** Set one layer on a cake plate or stand and cover with the icing. Repeat with remaining layers, then ice the sides of the cake. Place pecan halves around the top, if desired. Place the cake in the refrigerator and let it stand until the icing sets, about 1 hour.

The cake can be stored in an airtight container in the refrigerator for up to 5 days. If refrigerated, let the cake stand at room temperature for about 10 minutes before serving.

"I DON'T LIKE RED VELVET" RED VELVET CAKE

MAKES 8 TO 12 SERVINGS

If you don't like red velvet cake, it's because you've never had a good one. My grandmother's recipe rivals any I've had. This one's easy. Her recipe called for water or milk. I use chocolate milk to make it richer. For my from-scratch cream cheese icing, see page 234–235.

Softened butter and flour, to prepare the pans

1 (15.25-ounce) box yellow cake mix, such as Duncan Hines

1 (3.4-ounce) box instant vanilla or chocolate pudding mix

¼ cup unsweetened Dutch-processed cocoa powder

1 tsp vanilla extract

4 large eggs

½ cup neutral oil

1 cup chocolate milk, such as Yoo-hoo

1 (1-ounce) bottle red food coloring

Cream Cheese Icing (234–235)

Pecan halves, toasted, for garnish (optional)

1. **Make the cake:** Preheat the oven to 350°F. Butter 3 (8-inch) round cake pans and dust with flour.

2. In a large bowl, whisk the cake mix, pudding mix, and cocoa. In a separate bowl, whisk the vanilla, eggs, oil, chocolate milk, and food coloring. Pour the wet mixture into the dry ingredients and mix by hand or with an electric mixer on medium speed until just combined. Do not overmix. Divide the batter evenly among the prepared pans and smooth the tops.

3. Bake the cakes, spacing the cake pans evenly on the oven rack (don't let them touch), for about 15 minutes, or until the cakes barely shrink from the sides of the pan. Let cool on a wire rack for 15 minutes. Unmold the cakes onto parchment and place on wire cooling racks to cool for 15 to 20 minutes.

4. **Frost the cake:** Place one layer of the cake on a plate or cake stand and cover with the icing. Repeat with the remaining layers. Ice the sides of the cake, and place pecan halves around the top, if desired. Let the cake stand in the refrigerator until the icing sets, about 1 hour, before serving. Slice and serve.

The cake can be stored in the refrigerator in an airtight container for up to 5 days. If refrigerated, let the cake stand at room temperature for about 10 minutes before serving.

HD'S RYE APPLE PIE

MAKES ABOUT 6 TO 8 SERVINGS

I like to use a mixture of Honeycrisps and Granny Smiths for this pie. I *highly* recommend doubling the filling recipe and freezing the extra so you can quickly make another pie down the road. You can also use the cooked filling for easy fried pies or turnovers. I'm dedicating this one to Mark and Digger, my two favorite moonshiners.

APPLE PIE FILLING (MAKES ABOUT 3 CUPS)

6 large apples, peeled, cored, and cut into ½-inch wedges

1 T fresh lemon juice

1 ¼ cup apple juice

¼ cup Sugarland's Shine Mark and Digger's Rye Apple Moonshine, or apple juice

¼ cup packed light brown sugar

⅓ cup granulated sugar

2 T butter

1 ½ tsp ground cinnamon

⅛ tsp ground nutmeg

¼ tsp salt

1 ½ tsp cornstarch

½ tsp vanilla extract

¼ tsp butter flavoring

1 frozen deep-dish piecrust, thawed

CRUMBLE (FOR ONE PIE)

1 cup white cake mix or all-purpose flour

1 tsp ground cinnamon

¼ cup (½ stick) salted butter, room temperature

1. **Make the pie filling:** Preheat the oven to 400°F. Toss the sliced apples and lemon juice in a large saucepan and set aside.

2. In a medium saucepan or pot, combine the apple juice, moonshine, brown sugar, granulated sugar, butter, cinnamon, nutmeg, and salt. Cook over medium-high heat and stir gently until the butter is melted and the mixture is frothy. Pour over the apples and bring to a simmer over medium heat.

3. Cover the saucepan and reduce to medium-low heat, stirring occasionally, until apples are tender, about 15 to 20 minutes (if using very ripe or organic apples, reduce cooking time to 10 to 15 minutes).

4. In a small dish, whisk cornstarch with 1 to 2 tablespoons of the apple pie filling juice. Stir the cornstarch mixture into the apples while they're hot and bubbling, and simmer to thicken. Turn off the heat and allow the apple mixture to thicken and cool completely.

5. Once pie filling has cooled, stir in the vanilla and butter flavoring,

and pour the filling into an unbaked piecrust.

6. **Make the crumble topping:** In a medium mixing bowl, use a fork to combine the cake mix (or flour), cinnamon, and butter. Sprinkle the crumble over your pie, and bake the pie for 35 minutes. Tent the edges of the crust with strips of aluminum foil and continue baking for 5 minutes more. Let cool, about 20 minutes, and serve.

GETCHYO' MAN COCONUT CREAM PIE

MAKES 8 TO 10 SERVINGS

They've been divorced for over twenty years, but Daddy still requests this pie from Mama! Here's my version.

1 (7-ounce) bag sweetened coconut flakes

1 (14-ounce) can sweetened condensed milk

2 (3-ounce) boxes vanilla "Cook & Serve" pudding mix

4 large egg yolks

½ cup full-fat coconut milk, as needed

Pinch of salt

1 cup sour cream

1 frozen deep-dish piecrust, baked and cooled

1 ½ cups Better Than Whipped Cream (213)

1. Preheat the oven to 350°F. Spread the coconut on a baking sheet. Toast 4 to 5 minutes, until it's lightly browned. Stir it around in the pan and toast another 1 to 2 minutes. Watch it carefully. Coconut can burn like red headed children on the beach. Let it cool.

2. In a heavy medium saucepan or pot, whisk the condensed milk, pudding mix, yolks, coconut milk, and salt to combine. Cook over medium heat, whisking constantly, until it starts to bubble. Remove from the heat and stir in half of the coconut. Let the mixture cool completely. When cooled, fold in the sour cream and spread the filling in the baked piecrust.

3. Cover loosely with plastic wrap and chill for 4 hours or overnight. Serve with a dollop of homemade whipped cream. Sprinkle liberally with more toasted coconut.

The pie can be stored in an airtight container in the refrigerator for up to 4 days.

GETCHYO' MAN CHOCOLATE PECAN PIE

MAKES 8 TO 10 SERVINGS

Mother and I disagree on two things . . . the men I date and chocolate chips in your pecan pie. For me, it's like air conditioning—once you've had it, you don't wanna go back.

2 cups pecan halves

1 frozen deep-dish piecrust, thawed

⅔ cup chocolate chips

2 T all-purpose flour, divided

¼ cup (½ stick) salted butter, melted

1 cup plus 2 T packed light brown sugar

1 scant cup light corn or cane syrup

3 large eggs, lightly beaten

1 T Tennessee whiskey, such as Jack Daniel's

¾ tsp vanilla extract

¼ tsp salt

Dash ground cinnamon

1. Preheat the oven to 350°F. Coarsely chop about 1¼ cups of the pecans into square cubes (it makes the texture awesome) and sprinkle in the bottom of the piecrust. Set the remaining pecan halves aside for garnish. Toss the chocolate chips with 1 tablespoon of flour, shake off the excess flour, and sprinkle over the chopped pecans.

2. In a medium bowl beat the melted butter and brown sugar with an electric mixer on high speed for about 1 minute. Add the syrup, eggs, whiskey, vanilla, salt, cinnamon, and the remaining 1 tablespoon of flour, and mix until combined. Pour into the piecrust. Top with remaining pecan halves (make it pretty). Place the pie on a baking sheet.

3. Bake the pie for 25 minutes. Tent the edges of crust with strips of aluminum foil, and continue baking until the filling is puffed and jiggles as a unit when you gently shake the pan, about 25 minutes more. Let the pie cool completely. I prefer mine chilled. The pie can be refrigerated for up to 4 days. Serve with Better Than Whipped Cream (213).

PEANUT BUTTER PIE

MAKES 8 SERVINGS

It's a four-ingredient pie, Cheryl. Doesn't get easier than this. Substitute chocolate chips for the toffee peanuts if you wish.

8 ounces (1 block) cream cheese, softened

1 cup creamy or crunchy peanut butter

1 heaping cup powdered sugar

1 ½ cups Better Than Whipped Cream (213)

1 heaping cup coarsely chopped butter-toffee peanuts (or chocolate chips), optional

1 (9-inch) graham cracker or Oreo piecrust

1. In a large bowl, beat the cream cheese and peanut butter with an electric mixer on high speed until smooth. Then, on low speed, gradually beat in the powdered sugar. Use a silicone spatula to fold in the whipped cream. Fold in the peanuts (or chocolate chips), if using, and spread the filling into the piecrust. Smooth the top.

2. Refrigerate until chilled and set, at least 6 hours or preferably overnight. Slice and serve chilled.

The pie can be refrigerated for up to 3 days.

IN A DASH: Substitute a 12-ounce container of thawed frozen whipped topping (like Cool Whip) instead of whipped cream if you must.

EASY ALMOND TORTE

MAKES 12 TO 14 SERVINGS

This one's easy to memorize and make frequently for last-minute thank-yous and such. My mother makes this once a week.

- ¾ cup (1 ½ sticks) butter, softened
- 1 ½ cups sugar, plus 1 to 2 T for sprinkling
- 1 ½ cups all-purpose flour
- 2 large eggs
- ¼ tsp salt
- 1 tsp vanilla extract
- 1 tsp almond extract
- ¼ cup slivered almonds, for sprinkling

1. Preheat the oven to 350°F. Line an 8-inch ovenproof skillet (preferably cast iron) or 8-inch cake pan with aluminum foil. Grease the foil with butter.

2. In a medium bowl, cream the butter and sugar with an electric mixer on high speed until fluffy. Add the flour, eggs, salt, vanilla, and almond extract, and mix on medium speed just until the eggs are absorbed. Spread into the prepared skillet. Sprinkle the almonds on top with another tablespoon or two of sugar.

3. Bake until golden brown, for no more than 45 minutes (you'll think the cake's not done, but it will set once it's cooled). Let the cake cool completely before cutting. Cut into wedges and serve with coffee or fresh fruit and Better Than Whipped Cream (213).

Recipes

BUC-EE'S BLONDIES

MAKES 15 BLONDIES

I can't tell blondes apart from one another, but I never forget a blondie. This is my pathetic grab for a Buc-ee's endorsement.

2 cups all-purpose flour

1 T baking powder

1 tsp salt

1 cup (2 sticks) unsalted butter, melted

1 cup granulated sugar

1 cup packed brown sugar

2 large eggs

2 tsp vanilla extract

2 cups Sea Salted Caramel Beaver Nuggets (see Chef's Note)

1 cup white chocolate chips (optional)

1. Preheat the oven to 300°F. Lightly butter a 9 x 13-inch baking dish.

2. In a medium bowl, whisk the flour, baking powder, and salt together and set aside. In a separate medium bowl, using an electric mixer on high speed, beat the butter, granulated sugar, and brown sugar until creamy, about 2 minutes. One at a time, beat in each of the eggs, then the vanilla. Mix until smooth. With the mixer on low, gradually beat in the flour mixture until just combined.

3. Roughly chop 1 ½ cups of the Beaver Nuggets and leave the remaining nuggets whole. Fold in the chopped and whole Beaver Nuggets and white chocolate chips, if using. Scrape the batter into the prepared baking dish and smooth the top.

4. Bake the blondies until golden brown and set in the center, about 40 minutes. Transfer to a wire cooling rack and cool completely.

5. Cut into 15 equal pieces and serve.

The blondies can be stored in an airtight container at room temperature for up to 5 days.

CHEF'S NOTE

Buc-ee's Beaver Nuggets are like salted caramel corn but made with puffed corn instead of popcorn. You can substitute 2 cups coarsely chopped Spiced Candied Pecans (57).

ELVIS
ELVIS
1935-1977

ELVIS ECLAIR CAKE

MAKES 8 TO 10 SERVINGS

You can look at me and tell I'm an Elvis fan. He's why I wear big-collared shirts, rings on every finger, and my sunglasses indoors. I whipped this dish up in his honor. I make the pudding from scratch, but here's a shortcut variation for my city girls.

CAKE

2 (3.4-ounce) boxes of instant vanilla pudding mix

3 cups half-and-half

18 (2 sleeves) large graham crackers, as needed

2 cups Better Than Whipped Cream (213) or thawed frozen whipped topping, such as Cool Whip

¼ cup Skrewball Peanut Butter Whiskey, as needed

16 Nutter Butter Cookies (half of a 16-ounce package)

2 large ripe bananas, sliced

CHOCOLATE ICING

½ cup (1 stick) salted butter

8 large marshmallows

Scant ⅓ cup whole milk

2 cups powdered sugar

½ cup unsweetened cocoa powder

½ tsp vanilla extract

1. **Make the cake:** In a medium bowl, whisk to dissolve the pudding mix into the half-and-half (it'll be rich 'n' thick, like Randy Houser. Yummy). Set aside to thicken, 5 to 10 minutes.

2. Arrange half of the graham crackers in the bottom of a 9 x 13-inch baking dish, breaking as needed to fit.

3. Fold the whipped cream or Cool Whip into the pudding. Spread half of the pudding over the graham crackers. Pour the whiskey into a plate or pie dish. One at a time, quickly dip each side of the peanut butter cookies into the whiskey (do not soak them), shake off the excess, and arrange over the pudding. Top the cookies with the banana slices, then the remaining pudding. Top with the remaining graham crackers, breaking to fit as before.

4. **Make the icing:** In a medium saucepan over medium-low heat, melt the butter and marshmallows. Whisk in the milk to combine. Remove from the heat. In a separate bowl, sift the powdered sugar and cocoa together. Whisk this powdered sugar mixture into the saucepan until smooth. Stir in

the vanilla. Pour and spread the icing over the graham crackers. Refrigerate, uncovered, until set, at least 4 hours or overnight. Serve chilled.

After the topping is set, the cake can be covered with plastic wrap and refrigerated for up to 3 days.

CHOCOLATE FONDUE

MAKES 8 SERVINGS

This fondue is so good it'll get ya a proposal. If you don't have a fondue pot, see substitutions below. Dip some fruit, marshmallows, cookies, cubes of cake, or your boyfriend in it.

¾ cup half-and-half

2 cups semisweet chocolate chips

1 tsp vanilla extract

¼ cup coffee liqueur, such as Kahlúa, or more half-and-half

In a small saucepan, scald the half-and-half over medium heat (or in a microwave-safe bowl on high, about 2 minutes). Remove from the heat and add the chocolate chips without stirring. Let stand 5 minutes, then whisk until smooth. Whisk in the vanilla and the liqueur. Keep warm over low heat, and serve with your dippers.

CHEF'S NOTE

If you don't own a fondue pot, use a small pot with a butter warmer under it (with a votive candle) to keep the fondue warm. There are even mini Crock-Pots for dips and fondues. Use what you've got—this is low-fuss!

NAOMI'S POSSUM PIE

MAKES 10 TO 12 SERVINGS

In April '22, I was on the red carpet at the CMT Awards, glammed up in my biggest arena-sized wig. The Judds were being honored that night, and I was just tickled to be in the same room with them (huge fan). I could've *shit* when Wynonna came right up to me and told me how my videos had entertained them during quarantine. She asked if she could introduce me to her mom and grab a picture. Cameras flashed, and without missing a beat, Naomi said, "Bitch! You better snatch that wig off your head. I'm supposed to have the tallest hair here!" True story. Life made.

Sadly, Naomi died two weeks later. I'm dedicating this one to her and Wynonna. Naomi called it "Possum Pie." This is a good springtime or summertime dessert (Naomi used Cool Whip).

CRUST

1 ½ cups all-purpose flour

½ cup butter-flavored shortening, such as Crisco

½ cup (1 stick) salted butter, softened

½ cup chopped pecans

2 T granulated sugar

½ tsp salt

SECOND LAYER

12 ounces (1 ½ blocks) cream cheese, softened

1 ⅔ cups powdered sugar

½ tsp vanilla extract, preferably clear

2 ½ cups Better Than Whipped Cream (213) or whipped topping, such as Cool Whip, divided

THIRD LAYER

2 cups whole milk

⅔ cup heavy cream

2 (3.4-ounce) packages instant chocolate pudding mix

1. **Make the crust:** Preheat the oven to 350°F. In a medium bowl, combine the flour, shortening, butter, pecans, sugar, and salt together, using a fork. Wet your fingers and press the mixture evenly into the bottom of a 9 x 13-inch baking dish. Bake until lightly brown, 11 to 12 minutes. Set aside to cool.

2. **Make the second layer:** In a separate medium bowl, blend the cream cheese, powdered sugar, and vanilla with an electric mixer on high speed until smooth. Fold in half of the whipped cream to combine, and spread onto the cooled crust. Be sure that the mixture touches the walls of the dish to seal the edges.

3. **Make the third layer:** In a medium bowl whisk the milk, cream, and chocolate pudding mix until combined. Spread over the cream cheese layer. Top with the reserved whipped cream.

4. Cover and chill to set, at least 4 hours or overnight. Cut into squares and serve chilled.

Cooking Is Therapeutic

✣ ✣ ✣ ✣ ✣ ✣ ✣

Something about being in the kitchen slows the world down. For us hardworking dreamers whose goals may take a long time to come to fruition, the kitchen can render instant gratification. It's rewarding to see the fruits of your labor.

I remember being hungry in Nashville, not having any food in my fridge or pantry, living off the dollar menu until I was out of pennies (I'll never eat Taco Bell again—woof). I'm not rich by any means, but now, when I open the door to a stocked refrigerator, it fills my heart. I praise God for all of it—down to the cool retro utensils I use. I thank Him for the roof over my head and for the friends that are coming over to share a meal with me. I thank Him for you and that you read this book too.

You don't have to believe to be thankful for the hands that made your meal possible. But someone grew it, raised it, harvested it, hauled it, stocked it, and then cooked it. That alone is worth a pause. So bow your head with a grateful heart before your next meal. It's good energy, man.

Cooking is another way to praise God. And there's nothing more therapeutic than praising Him. Shondo!

ACKNOWLEDGMENTS

To the precious fan, follower, or friend reading this right now: Thank you for watching my videos, making my recipes, buying those concert tickets—and now, this book. Couldn't have done this without you, Shoog. Never forget: The joy you've found in watching me online or reading these pages? It all comes from one source ... (see the next thank-you).

To the Big Man, the King of Elvis, the Holy Fryer of the best fried chicken we'll ever taste: Thank You for using my gifts to feed folks—body and soul. Love Yew.

To my HarperCollins family: Thank you for believing in this project as much as I believe in Jesus—and for letting me keep the butter in the damn recipes.

To Reactor Media, thank y'all so much for taking all these fine photos of my food.

To my amazing parents: for introducing me to good food, for providing me with opportunities to learn to cook, for allowing me to mess up in the kitchen and try again. Thank you for teaching me efficiency—how to plan ahead, how to season food well, and how to put love in it. I love you both more than fried chicken itself.

To my family, blood and extended: Thanks for all the retro hand-me-downs no one else wanted and for the great recipes and cooking tips through the years. And a special thanks to my Aunt JoAnn Goldwire: Your influence has meant so much to my family—in the kitchen and beyond. Love you.

To my sister, Brittany, and my childhood friend, Lauren: Thanks for helping me through those late-night bouts of writer's block. Your humor, intelligence, and passion for good food continue to inspire me. Love yew.

To Taran and Josh—my little team that could. Thank you for working around the clock, around my crazy schedule, for keeping me and the band fed while I made this big ol' book. Your loyalty means the world.

Taran, you saint! You've earned your stripes, girl!

To my Sony Music Publishing fam: I don't know why you keep me around, but you do. Thanks for loving me through the hard years, for continuing to pitch my songs and believe in what I do.

To Wilson Emebonur, the best personal trainer on Earth—thanks for the sexy "guitar arms" I never thought I'd find.

To Kecia and Mandy, for all the love and resources you've poured into me so selflessly.

To Kayley, Kinley, Alicia, Emily Anne, Casey, Mercedes, and Amy: Thanks for covering me, for seeing me for me. Your friendship has made me a better human. Wes, Braden, Dom, and Ryan . . . I love yew hotties.

To the Romersas, for opening your beautiful home to cohost the photo shoot, for believing in me and in *Stand By Your Pan*.

INDEX

A

B

C

D

E

F

G

H

I

J

K

L

M

N

O

P

R

S

ABOUT THE AUTHOR

Hannah Dasher is what happens when Loretta Lynn and AC/DC have a TikTok baby. A Nashville-based country-rock artist, recipe-slingin' internet sensation, and Southern storyteller, Hannah has built a loyal following by keeping it real and delicious. Her viral *Stand By Your Pan* cooking series has fed millions—spiritually *and* literally—and her music has landed her on stages from the Grand Ole Opry to opening for Reba, Hank, and Skynyrd.

This is her first cookbook. Lord, help us all—it won't be her last.

@HANNAHDAMNDASHER

@HANNAHDASHER

@HANNAHDASHEROFFICIAL

WWW.HANNAHDASHER.COM

WSM
GRAND

SMASH
LYNYRD SKYNYRD